THE
ADVANCE
MAN

THE ADVANCE MAN

by Jerry Bruno and Jeff Greenfield

William Morrow and Company, Inc., New York   1971

To the memory

of

Jerry's mother and father

and to

Dorothy and Carol

Acknowledgments

Our thanks go to Oscar Dystel, who decided that there was a book worth doing; to Jim Tolan, John Treanor, Herb Schmertz, and the other advance men Jerry worked with; to the thousands of people in hundreds of towns who put their time and energy into some of the experiences this book talks about; to Jim Corcoran, Kate Brown, Joe Dolan, and Joel Swerdlow for their assistance; and to Victor Temkin of Bantam, and Howard Cady at Morrow. To Sister Marie Moran at Grace Institute, and Mrs. Beta Jacobs, our appreciation for their help in the transcriptions.

A special note of thanks must go to Bebe Wallau and to Roz Mazar, for their unbelievable patience and energy in helping this book to get born.

Jeff Greenfield

How does one describe feelings of appreciation when a dream is made to come true after weeks and weeks of talking about yourself, what you believe, and what you have done. It is great to see a readable version of what you have said and find it right.

All of these things were made possible by this one man, Jeff Greenfield.

I first met Jeff while I was working for Senator Robert Kennedy. He and I were worlds apart. In my book he was an "intellectual." This meant he was not one of my kind. But I was wrong, and I found that out when we traveled on the 1968 Presidential campaign of Robert Kennedy. There, the "team" had to live together. I realized that he understood me and what I was doing. I also discovered he was willing to work like a truck driver. He never hesitated to grab a bag or run an errand, even though he was there only to write speeches for R.F.K.

To tell you what a great guy Jeff is would be wrong, because in the years to come Jeff Greenfield will make his own mark, believe me.

My thanks to Jeff.

JERRY BRUNO
January 7, 1971

A Word About Jerry Bruno

He is built like a fire hydrant; he has the tact of a pulling guard; when confronting a local official standing between him and the prospect of a large turnout, he can be something less than pleasant.

But Jerry Bruno knows more about the way politics works in America than a dozen political science professors and a hundred pollsters. He knows how it works because he has seen it firsthand: from the plant gates at Kenosha, Wisconsin, to the eighty-five-day campaign of Robert Kennedy in 1968. He knows not only how to turn out a crowd, but what moves them, intrigues them, attracts them. He never went to school beyond the ninth grade—but talking politics with Jerry Bruno is like talking with one of those rare teachers who has forced you to see things you did not know you could see.

Bruno's response to politics is instinctive. He has a feel for the layout of a town or city; he knows what streets people will be drawn to for a motorcade or a rally. He can sense, rather than analyze, a candidate's ability to persuade an audience to accept his views. And perhaps most important, Jerry Bruno has learned never to take things for granted.

I remember talking with Jerry once about the Bay of Pigs invasion. He shook his head.

"John Kennedy forgot the one thing he always taught

me about advance. He took it for granted that the
generals and the CIA knew what they were talking
about." He smiled. "You could say it was bad advance.
They told Kennedy there'd be a crowd at the beach,
but nobody really knew a damn thing about it. And
nobody ever asked if it made any sense to *think* the
Cubans would want any part of it."

This is a book about some of the things Jerry Bruno
saw and lived through and learned about the way we
do politics in America. Some of it may seem ludicrous,
or a waste of time; some of it may suggest we should
run our campaigns differently. But for better or worse,
this is how it is done now. It is time that the people
who vote for political leaders know something more
than they do now about the process. I don't know
anyone who can tell them more about this part of
political life than Jerry Bruno.

JEFF GREENFIELD
March 1, 1971

Contents

THE
ADVANCE
MAN

A President Meets the People—
John Kennedy Goes West

It started for me in the middle of August, 1963, when
Kenny O'Donnell, President Kennedy's appointments
secretary and his political watchdog, called me to the
White House.

"The President is going to make a Western tour
in September. It's going to be a conservation trip. We
want to hit the small states we might not get to in
1964."

We talked about the trip for a while, and then John
Kennedy walked into the Fish Room from his office.

"You're planning the conservation trip?" he asked.
Yes, we said.

"I want the crowds—I want those crowds to be
there."

It was supposed to be a "non-political" trip: "to
inspect the nation's program for the conservation and
development of natural resources," was the way the
White House announced the trip. But everybody
knew better, including the press. For one thing, there
is no such thing as a non-political action by a President.
I don't care if he's inviting old people to Thanksgiving
dinner or dedicating a dam—it's political. A President's
movement is too controlled, too elaborate, to be done
without thinking about it. And when you start thinking,
you get to thinking about politics.

This trip to be made by Kennedy was especially po-

litical. By the fall of 1963, the political pace was beginning to speed up. It was already pretty clear that
Barry Goldwater was going to be Kennedy's opponent;
that Goldwater had popularity in the West; that Kennedy hadn't done at all well there in 1960, and that a
lot of Western Democratic senators were up for reelection. In those days, conservation and the environment weren't political issues to most Americans. So a
trip to promote conservation was a perfect excuse to go
to those states we might not get to in 1964.

"The President expressed the hope that this trip
would focus attention on this vital part of American
life and stimulate further efforts in the field of national
conservation," the White House press release said.
Well, maybe. But if they'd asked me to write the story,
it would have come out like this:

"The President expressed the hope that wildly enthusiastic crowds would greet him at every stop to
promise him their votes in 1964, and expressed the
hope that Bruno would pull those crowds out so that
his rear end would not wind up in a sling."

O'Donnell had given me the eleven states Kennedy
wanted to hit: Pennsylvania, Wisconsin, North Dakota,
Montana, Wyoming, Minnesota, Utah, Arizona, California, Idaho, and Nevada. The Interior Department
had come up with a long list of possible sites: national
parks, dams, reclamation projects, you name them. But
because the whole point of the trip was to prove John
Kennedy's support out West, it was left to me to figure
out where the President should go.

The first step was to consult with the Democratic
senators in the states Kennedy would visit. By some
amazing coincidence, nine of the eleven states had
incumbent Democrats who were coming up for reelection in 1964. We set up temporary shop in the office of
Mike Mansfield, the Democratic Majority Leader. We
met with them one by one; I'd learned years before
that you just can't pull everyone together in one room
for a general discussion about a campaign appearance,

because all you'll get is pulling and tugging from each person. I remember the discussion mostly because it offered me one of the really warm moments in politics.

Before I'd left the White House, Kennedy had said he wanted to visit Mansfield's father, who was ill. I told that to Mansfield, and he just looked stunned.

"Did the President really say that?" he asked.

"Yes, he did," I said.

For a minute I thought he was going to cry. Finally he looked up.

"Would you thank him for me?" Mansfield said. "Tell him I really appreciate that."

After you spend about six thousand man-hours dealing with so many fourth-rate sons of bitches in politics, you recognize who really is a decent guy. Mansfield is one of the best, and it was good to give some welcome news to a nice guy instead of playing ego massage with a guy you wouldn't spend five minutes with if you didn't have to.

With the consultation done, with the names of dozens of contacts in each possible site given to us by the senators, we began plotting out the trip. We did it the only way possible: by taking Air Force One and going into every state the President planned to visit, getting ideas, looking around, seeing firsthand what problems would arise if the President went here or there or the other place. It's a long, tiring process. But there's no other way to do advance, whether for a candidate or a President. If you don't see each place with your own eyes, if you don't know how people can get to a speaking site, if you don't know how to set up a stop to get a crowd and to make the crowd you get look bigger than it is, you're dead.

And every place we hit, we found the same problem —getting impressive crowds. It's one thing to run a motorcade through the middle of Chicago at high noon and get a huge turnout. If you count right, Harold Stassen can claim he drew 250,000 people, since they're all standing there waiting for the light to change. But the thing about conservation sites is that they're *away* from people. When you get right down to it, that's the whole point of national parks and campsites. And dam-sites aren't often found in the middle of a city.

Now if John Kennedy were going on a fishing trip, that would be great. But John Kennedy wasn't going on a fishing trip. And lovely pictures of Kennedy sur-rounded by clear blue skies and miles of open spaces were not exactly what we had in mind. So as we began setting up the trip, the problem of where to put John Kennedy became central. One site solved itself—the Gifford Pinchot Institute in Milford, Pennsylvania. We found a clearing with a clump of tall pine trees in the background. By setting the President's speech there, we "packed them in," if you can pack people in outdoors. The same crowd in a wide, open field would have looked pathetically small.

For the rest of the trip, we hit on a more or less consistent solution: high-school football stadiums and field houses, county fairgrounds, and in some cases, college field houses. (Why no big university football stadiums? Because they're almost impossible to fill, as you'll see. I don't try to press my luck.)

For the President's trip to Duluth, Minnesota, we would substitute the University of Minnesota-Duluth Physical Education Building. For Kennedy's stop in Billings, Montana, we would send him to the Yellow-stone County Fairgrounds. For the trip to Great Falls, Montana, a high-school football stadium. It was in Montana, I think, that a few of the local people thought it would be great if Kennedy would speak about Yel-low Trail Dam and pay it a visit.

"Fine," I said, "but we'll do it at this high-school football field."

"Why a football stadium?" someone asked.

"Security," I think I said.

It was easy enough to establish the logistics for this kind of stop. If Kennedy was supposed to dedicate a dam, we'd rig up a button to the speaker's stand at

the field house or stadium. One push of the button, and
the first dynamite charge would go off. But we realized
that it could get a little embarrassing if Kennedy never
saw a tree or lake in this conservation tour. In fact, as
we began moving in the direction of crowds and away
from scenic areas, the conservation people got a little
bothered.

"Listen, Bruno," one of them said. "We just want you
to know we know what you're doing."

"Well," I said, "if you know what I'm doing, then let
me do it." My good nature and calm, absolutely even
temper are always at their finest when somebody starts
giving me trouble as I'm trying to work out a campaign
or political stop. But Andy Hatcher, the Assistant
White House Press Secretary, also suggested that we
had to mix it up a bit; that going into nothing but
stadiums and field houses would make the politics of
the trip too obvious.

In the course of mapping out Kennedy's route, I
had a chance to give myself two enormous ego boosts,
and I took both chances. First, we were flying from
Milford, Pennsylvania, to Ashland, Wisconsin. As we
were passing over Milwaukee, I went up to the cabin.

"Could you go just a little south?" I asked the pilot,
and he changed course a fraction. In a minute we were
over Kenosha, Wisconsin, my hometown. It was absolutely clear, and even flying at 28,000 feet I could just
make out the American Motors plant where I'd been
working as a forklift operator six years earlier. If they
could see me now, I thought, I know exactly what
they'd say:

"Bruno, you phony bastard, get off the President's
plane and get back here."

The second personal kick I got came at Great Falls,
Montana. In a lot of places in the less crowded states
and areas of America, the only place where the President's plane can land is at an Air Force base, and that
was the case in Great Falls. Now whenever anybody
important lands, an Air Force commander will get a

funny feeling all over. It's a chance to do something real, instead of playing war. When a *President* lands, it can take up a month with full preparations for military honors, color guard, review of the troops, the whole routine. You could tie up a whole base staff for weeks, thinking about the plans, drawing up the charts, rolling up maps, unrolling maps, and generally having a wonderful time.

The only trouble was, John Kennedy hated military pageants—with a passion. And his brother Robert hated them even more. I'm not sure why. Partly it had to do with the fact that pomposity really bothered them; partly it was that they wanted to prove they could handle crowds and events on a basis of personal strength, and somehow all that brass and pomp blocked their own roles; partly I think they saw in the military and police a kind of arrogance, a sense that in these kinds of situations there was always a swagger around.

Anyway, my instructions were absolutely clear that Kennedy "did not want one single military review on the whole trip." And, as we land in Great Falls, there's the commanding general waiting to meet Air Force One.

We walk into this enormous briefing room which is absolutely jammed with charts and maps and lists of where the President's plane is going to land and how long the review is going to be. There must be forty-five assorted colonels and captains and God knows what else standing around waiting for this event. If the Russians had been in Billings that week, I don't know what we'd have done. And you have to remember, I came out of the Navy in World War II, strictly an enlisted man deck-swabber type. I still remember all the things we told each other we'd do to those big shots if we ever had the chance.

I also remembered, on a more political thought, that Mike Mansfield's contact for me at this stop was the local sheriff, John Krsul. Only he's not to be seen. And

I should have known, because as the general began to talk I started looking around for the sheriff.

"You're not very interested, Mr. Bruno," the general said after a minute. And I kept looking around, trying to locate the sheriff.

"I can't find somebody I'm looking for," I said.

"You're not very interested in the outline for this review," the general said again.

"To tell you the truth, General, I'm looking for the sheriff," I said. And he didn't look at all pleased.

"What do you want the sheriff for?" he asked, and all those days in the Navy came back, and all those promises.

"Because he's the guy I want to talk to about this trip," I said, and then I raised my voice and shouted to the room, "Is the sheriff in the crowd?" And way in the back of the room, so jammed in I couldn't even see him, came this voice: "Bruno, here I am."

"Come on up here," I shouted.

The general's color wasn't very good at all. You should see purple and khaki-green mixed some time.

"You can't do that," he said. "We have to tell you what the President's going to do when he arrives."

"Let me just stop a minute," I said, and I was really quiet at this point. You don't know what that means unless you remember that I shout "Good morning" to people.

"All of this doesn't mean anything," I started again, "because we're not going to do it. Any of it."

"What do you mean, you're not going to do it? What do you mean?" the general said, really angry.

"Just what I said. We're landing here. We want no honors. No parades. No nothing. The sheriff is running this trip. He is making all local decisions."

It was beginning to sound like a service comedy, and I guess we had to play it out that way.

"This is unheard of," the general shouted. "Who is this man?"

"I'll see you," I said. "Let's go, Sheriff. Show me where the stadium is."

John Krsul and I got up, and forty-five officers and several hundred man-hours of charts and papers and outlines just stood and sat there as we left. I figured they'd be upset, but what the hell, President Kennedy was always talking about civilian control of the military.

A much more shaky episode with the military came during another leg of the planning for Kennedy's Western swing. We were trying to figure out where Kennedy could go in northern California, and were told about a forest area south of San Francisco that had been suggested as a site for a national park. Nearby was an open-air Greek theater that would be perfect for crowds and for a speech by the President. So Jerry Behn, in charge of White House Secret Service, and I took a helicopter and went looking for a place to land. We found what looked like a perfect spot and went in and landed.

Behn and I got out and looked around, and for a minute or two we couldn't tell where we were. Then we sort of figured it out together.

"Hey," one of us said to the other, "this is a military base." And sure enough, a jeep came along with a soldier in it, a fellow named Sgt. McSweeney.

"We're from the White House," I said. "Can we get a ride to Headquarters?"

"Sure," McSweeney said, and we went along to Headquarters. No checks, no identification, just like that.

"Can we see the commander?" I asked when we got to Headquarters. "We're with the White House."

"Right away," somebody said, and in we went!

We introduced ourselves, and then Behn asked the commander, "Could you tell us where we are?"

"Sure," he said. "This is the 666th Radar Squad, Mill Valley, California."

"Jesus Christ," I muttered to Behn. "This is our first line of defense. We land a helicopter here, no clearance, nobody spots us, and here we are talking to the commander and we *still* haven't shown anybody our identification."

I always thought I understood the Bay of Pigs much clearer after that episode.

With these fond memories, I headed back to Washington and the White House Fish Room to go over the details of the trip with Kenny O'Donnell. It was an elaborate job, as any Presidential trip is, with all the questions that give an advance man fits, like who gets to introduce the President, who gets to introduce the man who introduces the President, who sits on the podium, who meets him at the airport. And almost every senator had a special side trip he wanted Kennedy to make—to visit this schoolgirl, this site, this depressed area. Each of them would "only take five minutes." Put together, they would have added a week to the trip and cost unbelievable amounts of money and time. That's how complicated it is for a President to go anywhere.

As Kenny and I were working out the arrangements, President Kennedy walked in.

"How's it going?" he asked, and for five minutes he peppered us with questions. I never saw anybody work like John Kennedy: if there was something you didn't know or hadn't thought about, that was always the first question he asked.

"What do you think?" he asked finally.

"I think it may be screwed up," I said. "We've got all these places out from nowhere, and I don't know how the crowds are going to be."

"Well, I want those crowds. Maybe we should cancel the trip," the President said.

"No, I think we can do it."

"Well, you'd better be accurate," Kennedy said, leaving. "Lots of luck."

"Bruno," Kenny said, "I hope you're making the President look good."

Now in all honesty, I'd learned to always play down a political trip. If I thought we could turn out ten thousand people at an airport, I'd tell Kennedy we'd be lucky to get five thousand. It made me look good, and it also sparked him when he got a bigger crowd than we'd figured on. But I also just didn't know how we'd do out West. Between all the talk about Goldwater and the John Birch Society, I was uncertain. So we began using the machinery to help pull crowds.

Local advance men would visit school principals and Boards of Education, explaining how rare it was for a President to visit their town and what a great opportunity it was for the children of North Dakota or Utah to hear a President speak. Wouldn't it be a good idea to cancel classes? Congressmen and senators played up the visit prominently in their newsletters and mailings—free, thanks to the franking privilege for "non-political" mailings (that's when the newsletter doesn't say "Vote for Me"). Local newspapers and college papers were giving out information on motorcade routes, schedules, and advance stories. All we had to do now was to wait for the crowds.

On September 24, 1963, Air Force One took off from Andrews Air Force Base for Milford, Pennsylvania, the first stop on the eleven-state tour. The plane was filled with senators, congressmen, and conservation officials. After about ten minutes, Kennedy came out of his compartment and began greeting people. I was sitting with a freshman Pennsylvania congressman, and the President, looking very solemn, came over, bent down, and whispered in my ear. I looked up and said, "It's going to be O.K., Mr. President."

The congressman looked incredulous. For what piece of vital advice had he asked me? He had said, "Is the trip still screwed up?"

Looking back on it, the trip in one sense could have been screwed up, but not because of any failure in planning. The crowds were big and mostly friendly, the sites were right, but through the first stops—Milford, Ashland, Wisconsin, Duluth, Minnesota, and Grand Forks, North Dakota—the crowds were unresponsive and restless. In a political trip, it isn't enough to draw crowds. You have to touch them somehow, to leave them with a sense of excitement. And that just wasn't happening. Kennedy would reach, he would try different themes, but the sense of emotional attachment just wasn't there.

It all changed in Billings, Montana. The President was introducing Mike Mansfield, and he also said a kind word about Senator Ev Dirksen, the Minority Leader, for his work in getting the Test Ban Treaty through the Senate. It had been passed a short time earlier, mostly because Dirksen carried enough Republicans along with him.

And for the first time the crowd cheered, really cheered. And then in Great Falls, Montana, he said a few more words about peace—about how all of this beauty wouldn't be worth much if our children weren't going to live to enjoy it. And again there was cheering and real enthusiasm.

The turning point, I guess, was Salt Lake City, Utah. This was supposed to be solid Goldwater country: conservative, even a little pro-Birch Society. But for this stop Kennedy had a prepared speech, planned because of the enthusiasm for his ad lib statements on peace and the Test Ban Treaty. It was a full-fledged attack on the Goldwater view of the world; about the need to step back from the danger of nuclear war.

I didn't hear the speech, because I was a block away from the Mormon Tabernacle, getting ready to make the telephone calls to Tacoma, Washington, to inquire how things were going there. But in a way I heard the speech. I heard the loudest cheers I can remember hearing for the President. I heard them interrupt the speech with applause and cheering so loud that I think the whole Tabernacle shook (that was when Kennedy talked about the radiation, the dangers to our children, and how we were trying to stop that). I just stopped what I was doing and listened to the sounds. All I knew then was that whatever the President was saying, he was getting an incredible reception for Utah.

I saw Evelyn Lincoln, his secretary, later and asked her how he was feeling.

"Jerry," she said, "he is very, very happy."

And he proved it in two ways. First, he invited me at the end of the trip to come up to Bing Crosby's home in Palm Springs, California, where he was relaxing. It was something he almost never did, and to people working for any important man, that kind of invitation means something special. He was in the pool, just relaxing, and he kept asking me how we'd gotten so many people out. I kept telling him, "It's because they really like you, Mr. President," and he'd say, "Knock it off, it's not that." It was the kind of teasing he did when he was really happy.

And then a few days after we got back to Washington, I got a letter from the President.

Dear Jerry,
The Western trip represented an outstanding job of organization and planning. Please accept my warmest thanks.

> With every good wish,
> Sincerely,
> John F. Kennedy

It was the only letter, the only written kind of thanks, I'd ever gotten from John Kennedy. And thinking about it, you wonder what would happen if Presidents and candidates did what some people think they're doing, if they never really got out and saw people, if they relied on TV and press conferences and staged events, if they didn't have to test their appeal and their thoughts face-to-face with voters. Would John Kennedy have ever known that peace was on the minds of all Americans, whether conservative or liberal? Would he have decided to run in 1964 on a pledge of peace and disarmament? How could the best advisers in the world have shown him what he saw and heard —that this was what people wanted now. I don't think they could have.

For all of the pulling and tugging we did, for all of our own work to draw crowds, it was Kennedy and people, face-to-face, that meant something real and different might have happened in this country. But we never got the chance to find out.

What I Do—and Why

It was in Ohio in the fall of 1960, shortly after John Kennedy's first television debate with Richard Nixon. The day hadn't been going well. We were several hours late, stuck in a monumental traffic jam, with political dignitaries missing or unaccounted for, and a very disgusted candidate, a very disgusted governor of Ohio, Mike DiSalle, and a very unhappy aide, me.

Kennedy turned to nobody in particular. "I wonder how Hannibal ever made it across the Alps?" he said.

"It was easy," Governor DiSalle said, looking over at me. "He didn't have an advance man."

I'm an advance man.

It's my job in a campaign to decide where a rally should be held, how a candidate can best use his time getting from an airport to that rally, who should sit next to him and chat with him quietly in his hotel room before or after a political speech, and who should be kept as far away from him as possible.

It's also my job to make sure that a public appearance goes well—a big crowd, an enthusiastic crowd, with bands and signs, a motorcade that is mobbed by enthusiastic supporters, a day in which a candidate sees and is seen by as many people as possible—and at the same time have it all properly recorded by the press and their cameras.

I'm almost never there when a speech is being

made, because I'm figuring out how to get the candidate from the hall to his next appearance as effectively as possible. Or I'm calling to another city to find out why the high-school band isn't already waiting at the airport, or why the automobile dealer has decided not to lend us twelve cars for our triumphant motorcade into town. Or maybe I'm trying to convince the press that those twenty thousand people who met us in downtown Cleveland were really fifty thousand, or that the empty streets in front of the hotel were empty because we urged people not to show up there—not because nobody cared about the candidate.

I've been doing this kind of political work for fifteen years, more or less. From handing out leaflets in a snowstorm in Wisconsin to planning a state visit by a President to Naples, Italy, I've been there. In that time I've probably insulted as many people and made as many enemies as it's possible to think of. I've had a mayor call a press conference to denounce me as a "New York gutter rat," I've been labeled a Mussolini, and there are dozens of towns in America where I don't think I'll ever show my face again.

But I've worked that way because, when you're part of a political campaign, the stakes are as high as they come, and there just isn't any time. I think sometimes it's what fighting a war or playing a pro football game is like: you've got one chance to win votes in this town at this time. If you make one slip, one mistake, it can ruin a day, a week, of campaigning; it can make enough difference to turn an election, and if you want to get really dramatic about it, it can determine who leads this country.

As much as anything else, the crowds John Kennedy got in the last weeks of the 1960 campaign turned that election, because the energy, the excitement, was with Kennedy, not Nixon. Those crowds came in large measure because Kennedy was something new and exciting in American political life. But they also came because a lot of people like me were working our

heads off to give them the chance to come out; we
were using every device we could to create an appearance that people would want to see.

Between the people who talk about the circus atmosphere of campaigns and the people who warn
about the danger of assassination, this kind of campaigning is in a kind of disrepute. The idea now for
some people seems to be to put a candidate on TV
with as much money as you can find, stage a few appearances for the cameras and newsmen, and keep
your strength up for press conferences by keeping
your distance from the people.

Maybe it's because that kind of politics would put
me out of work, but I'm convinced that we can't stop
personal, face-to-face campaigning. I think—and I
hope I can show—how vital it is both for people and
for potential Presidents, senators, congressmen, gov-
ernors, and mayors. Because once we get through with
all our tricks and gimmicks, it still becomes one man
facing people he wants to lead. It's up to him to prove
himself, to listen to people, to hear what's on their
minds, to learn also how to speak to them in ways they
can understand.

Recently somebody sent me the secret manual for
Nixon's advance team in 1968. It spells out what they
think an advance operation means. In one place it
says:

> The central point of scheduling is that cam-
> paigning is symbolic, i.e., it is not what the can-
> didate actually does as much as what it appears
> he does.

I happen to think that's a dangerous notion, and one
that perfectly describes Richard Nixon's whole style
—to *appear* to be campaigning while what he's really
doing is going through a phony stage show with no
real contact. I also think it's stupid, that people can
and do see through it. After all the kidding around

stops, it's what a candidate *really* does that makes the difference.

Maybe I feel the way I do because of the way I got into politics. Today the route seems to be through law school or public relations. My own start was a lot different.

I was born in 1926 in Kenosha, Wisconsin. My parents were immigrants from Cosenza, Italy. They came here to find work. And they found it—for three months out of every year. In the eight or nine months that my father did not find work at a foundry, the whole family, including all seven of us kids, used to pick onions in the fields: something like migrant workers, only we had a permanent home.

(In 1963, when I was in Naples advancing President Kennedy's trip, I went by train and cable car to visit Cosenza in the mountains of southern Italy. I found my uncle and his twelve children living in two rooms of a barn, working as a laborer for the *patrone.* I'd have been doing the same thing if my folks had stayed in Italy.)

I dropped out of school in the ninth grade, because during the Depression all of us worked when and where we could find it. During World War II I tried to enlist in the Navy and was kept out for medical reasons. Finally, in 1945, they let me in. I didn't see any action, and served on a couple of battleships until I was discharged in 1947. With some friends I hitch-hiked across the country to look around.

One event stands out: a night in Trenton, New Jersey, when we ran out of money and the police let us spend the night in jail. I remember it because in the fall of 1960 I went into New Jersey to meet with Governor Meyner about Kennedy's campaign. A police escort was waiting to take me to the Governor's Mansion, and I found myself riding with the chief of the state police. I complimented him on his facilities.

I went back to Wisconsin and settled down in Kenosha, where in 1952 I found myself working for Amer-

ican Motors, driving a forklift truck. I drove supplies
from the receiving dock to the workers on the assem-
bly line. And that's what I'd be doing today if it
wasn't for a friend named Mario Giombetti, who
owned a TV repair shop, but who wasn't even a
millionaire. We used to go to Pete's Bar after work for
a beer or two. One night Mario mentioned that there
was a political meeting in the room above the bar.
More out of boredom than anything else, I went up-
stairs and saw William Proxmire—a former state legis-
lator who was planning to run for governor in 1954.
For some reason, I asked him a couple of questions,
and he seemed interested. In fact, we talked for a
while.

Right there, I learned something I never forgot. This
guy Proxmire was somebody I'd never met and never
really heard of. But he looked like he cared about
what I was asking. He took the time to explain something to me, and he finished by asking me to help him
run for governor in any little way I could. That meant
a hell of a lot. Nobody had ever asked me what I
thought of anything before. I couldn't imagine how
anybody running for governor could need my help, but
Proxmire had taken the trouble to *ask*—and that was
enough for me. It was something I remembered years
later when I'd hear John Kennedy or Robert Kennedy
say: "I ask for your help," or, "With your help, we can
make this effort work." That's what they were doing
instinctively, the same way William Proxmire pulled
me into politics: by asking for my help.

I was with Proxmire more or less from 1953 until
he finally got elected to the United States Senate in
1957, to fill out the term of Joe McCarthy, who had
died. I kept my job at American Motors, because Proxmire could in no way afford to pay me for any of my
work, even during his campaigns, much less in the
political "off-season." But I'd pass out leaflets in front
of plant gates and football stadiums, where Proxmire
loved to campaign. (It became a contest between

Estes Kefauver and him as to who shook the most hands.) He lost for governor in 1954, as he'd lost in 1952, and the day after he announced that he'd run again in 1956. In that year, I took a leave of absence to work on his campaign, and I earned my keep by standing up at union meetings and rallies and selling political buttons for a dollar. I managed to raise money for the campaign and keep myself alive at the same time. Meanwhile I'd started to get a little interested in political issues, which happens when you work for candidates. (Maybe you should be interested in issues first, then people, but for me, at least, it worked the other way.) For instance, I spent eight weeks on the picket line during the long, historic strike against the Kohler Company. I got on the Political Action Committee of my UAW local (it was a great way to get out of the plant for political work once a week). I even ran for county supervisor three times. Once Proxmire came down to pass out *my* leaflets, but I still lost.

Finally, in 1957, Proxmire won the Senate seat by more than 100,000 votes, and by that time I'd become one of his top aides, mostly by seniority. I was never much at issues or anything like that. But I'd always be there to help set up rallies, to go with him and help pass out literature, and I suppose I must have spent hundreds of days watching and listening to people and a politician. I think some of it sank in.

In 1957 I also was a kind of liaison man in helping to set up an important political event. The Democrats had only a one-seat edge in the Senate, and Washington thought it was a critical Senate race. So the Democratic Senatorial Campaign Committee decided we needed a campaigner to help us in the Polish-Catholic wards of Milwaukee. The man they sent was Senator John Kennedy of Massachusetts.

Kennedy came into Milwaukee, touring Polish neighborhoods with Congressman Clement Zablocki, who'd lost to Proxmire in the Senate Primary. It was a mixed-up affair in a lot of ways. For example, Prox-

mire has always been a kind of lone wolf, and he didn't
want to campaign with Kennedy, even though Kennedy was coming in to help him—I guess he was
already looking ahead to 1960 and didn't want to get
caught up in any Presidential politicking. But I remember that Kennedy was a very young-looking, very
attractive kind of candidate, with something about him
—a sense of class. He never got openly upset about
Proxmire's refusal to campaign with him, and he
carried the day off very well.

After Proxmire's election as senator, I became his
"Wisconsin secretary," handling a lot of casework:
that's work where a senator tries to help people who've
been shafted by different government agencies. If a
widow hasn't gotten her social security check, if a
soldier isn't being given a hardship discharge, people
usually ask their congressman or senator for help. We
opened a Wisconsin office to help people out in these
matters. When I wasn't doing that kind of work, I was
helping to mend political fences and doing advance
work for the upcoming election to the full six-year
term.

Proxmire won that election easily, and then closed
the Wisconsin office and brought me to Washington
as a political worker. It was two weeks after I'd ar-
rived there, in January of 1959, that I was riding to a
Senate office in the underground electric railroad and
happened to find myself sitting next to John Kennedy.

"You're Jerry Bruno," Kennedy said, although it was
almost two years since the one time I'd met him. He
recounted, with astonishing accuracy, what had happened on his trip to Milwaukee, and then he turned to
another subject.

"What about Wisconsin?" he said. "How do you
think I'd do there if I ran in the primary?" I said that
he'd made a good showing in 1957, and that was the
end of our conversation. But when I ran in to him
again in the halls outside the Senate Labor Committee, he asked me some questions about Wisconsin

politics and asked me to come see him the next morning at his house in Georgetown.

I think I had the same feeling about John Kennedy that I'd had about Proximire the first time I'd met him: a sense of disbelief that this wealthy, glamorous man who was thinking about running for President actually gave a damn about what I thought of anything, much less Presidential politics. I know I was flattered, and I suppose that was part of what made me as excited as I was the next morning—so excited, in fact, that I got there a half hour before our breakfast meeting and sat in my car until 9 A.M.

I was nervous as hell when I walked into the house and said hello to Kennedy. I'd had experience in Wisconsin working in a Senate race, but talking about the Presidency, that was something else. But after the third question or so, Kennedy made me forget that. He wanted hard facts; and it was unbelievable how much he knew about the state, the political lineups, Hubert Humphrey's strength, and where everyone stood in the political arena.

It was then that Kennedy suggested I go to work full time for him, organizing Wisconsin in case he decided to run in that state's primary. There was no doubt that he was running for President, at least not in any conversation I ever remember having. The only questions were what primaries he was going to run in. Looking back on it, I suppose he was interested in me for a couple of reasons: first, I was identified as a "Proxmire man," and that might mean something in the state; second, just from doing all that work with Proxmire I'd learned about Wisconsin politics and built up contacts; and third, my background was with labor and labor was thought to be strongly pro-Humphrey.

John and Robert Kennedy sized you up very quickly. If there was something about you they thought O.K., then your background and education and all the rest really didn't matter. If I'd ever had to send in a résumé to an organization, I would never have been considered for a job in a Presidential campaign. But because of an acccidental meeting, I found myself resigning from Proxmire's staff in the middle of June, 1959, and going back to Wisconsin to set up statewide Kennedy clubs.

That was the beginning; starting in late 1959, I got involved with advance work full time. Looking back on it now, it seems incredible that we ever got through that 1960 campaign in one piece. But I did, and I learned.

Learning the Ropes:
A Worm's-Eye View of the 1960 Campaign

Sometime in the middle of 1960, a typewriter repair shop could have made a fortune selling a special key a reporter could press and produce the phrase, "the well-oiled Kennedy machine." People had a weird sense of this incredible organization with unlimited money and power, coolly plotting every move to get John Kennedy nominated.

Well, all I can say is that the stuff that oiled most of my work was chaos and panic. The first thing a staff man had to be able to do with John Kennedy was to react when all hell broke loose, when all the careful plans went berserk, and when there was no time to check with anybody. I remember reading about the way Richard Nixon's campaign went like clockwork, and I kept thinking back to 1960, and how the "well-oiled Kennedy machine" put together campaign stops.

Take the first one I ever did, in November, 1959. Kennedy was supposed to come into Eau Claire, Marshfield, and then hit a few towns until he got to Milwaukee. We planned to have him speak at a fund-raising dinner in Marshfield for the state Democratic party. What we *didn't* know was that Richard Nixon was planning to speak just thirty miles away at a Republican dinner. Before we had the chance to think about whether we were ready to go head-to-head against the Vice-President in Republican territory, the local Democratic organization announced Kennedy's appearance, and there just was no way to gracefully back out.

John Kennedy was incredibly conscious of these kinds of situations. It became an absolute priority to outdraw Nixon, because Kennedy could sense what it took me years to learn: that there was some sort of a connection in people's minds between crowd appeal and leadership ability, as though they could sense that if a man couldn't draw people to hear him, and couldn't demonstrate that people cared about him, he couldn't win enough confidence to get elected.

Anyway, I moved up to Marshfield weeks before the dinner, and we pulled out all the stops. We told Humphrey and Stevenson supporters—truthfully—that this was money being raised for the Democratic party, not for Kennedy. We convinced them that we had to outdraw Nixon, since he was going to be the opponent no matter whom we nominated. We had labor committees, women's committees, committee committees—and every day there'd be a call from Kennedy to find out how the ticket sales were going. And, by God, we did outdraw Nixon in November, 1959, and the press wrote it up that way.

But anybody who thinks there was a committee of geniuses that figured out we could go one up on Nixon with this dinner should have seen us sweat for two months to make this turnout a success. It was an accident—just like most things in politics are.

Or take another example—during Kennedy's next trip to Wisconsin in late 1959. We were scheduled to go from Duluth, Minnesota, into Superior, Wisconsin, which is right across the border. Even as a novice, I'd learned to check details—I thought—and I made sure that our Superior trip was scheduled the day *after* one of the biggest high-school football games in the state, featuring the kind of rivalry where the whole town shuts down to watch the game. We got to Superior High School, and the hall was one-third filled.

I couldn't believe it. You could just see Kennedy's spirits flag. I saw then that the crowds were important, not just for politics, but because they did something for him. If he felt people in a town didn't care about him enough to come out and listen to him, his enthusiasm would just fade.

I was frantic. I ran around, livid, looking for one of our local friends.

"Where *is* everybody?" I screamed.

"At the football game," he said.

"The *football* game?" I yelled. "The football game was yesterday!"

"Nope," he said. "Rained out. We put it off a day."

"I want to talk to you, Jerry," somebody else said. I turned around. It was Kennedy.

"Where was the crowd?" he asked. I explained.

His voice got very cold and hard. "Whenever you plan any appearances," he said, "make absolutely sure of the details. Don't ever, ever schedule another appearance until you know all the facts and you make sure every detail's been completed."

I never forgot those words, and they changed the way I worked in politics from then on. I never tried to explain to people why I was making phone calls up to fifteen minutes before a political appearance, or why I'd want to know the name of every driver who was driving a car in a motorcade. But the real reason was that I was hearing those words of Kennedy's: ". . . make absolutely sure of the details."

That's why, whenever anybody asks me who taught me about advance work in politics, I always tell him John Kennedy. Because it's true. If there was ever a detail I left out, ever a question I couldn't answer, he'd always be sure to spot it when he checked out our preparations for a campaign stop. I forced myself to start anticipating the kind of thing Kennedy would ask me. And that way I started to learn how to ask myself details about campaigning: How did I know there'd be a loudspeaker there? Who was making telephone calls to tell people about a stop? Where was the band coming from? Who else or what else was going to be in town at the same time? All these details got to be second nature, because I always felt John Kennedy was looking over my shoulder.

Kennedy also showed me something else about politics, something that's always misunderstood. And that's how to be tough—or, if you like, ruthless. I always got a laugh out of the notion that it was Bobby Kennedy who was the ruthless one while John Kennedy was nice and relaxed. The fact is that it was Bobby who couldn't fire anybody, and John Kennedy who'd just get rid of somebody if he wasn't any good. And it was John Kennedy who showed me how to do it.

I even remember the date. It was January 21, 1960, at the Milwaukee County Labor Council. Labor was a crucial factor in any Democratic primary, and Humphrey had an edge here. He'd always been considered a friend of labor, and John Kennedy had been on the Labor Committee that investigated the Teamsters Union. His brother Bob had been general counsel to that Committee—and his pursuit of Hoffa had left some bad feeling. Most of the state's labor leaders were for Humphrey. And while Kennedy wasn't expecting an endorsement, he knew that a labor endorsement of Humphrey would really hurt his own chances.

So when Kennedy met with the leaders of the Labor Council, there was very little smiling and very little charm. He was tough and flat out.

"I don't expect an endorsement from labor," he said. "Neither do I expect them to endorse Humphrey. I sit on the Senate Labor Committee," he said, "and whether I win or lose, I will be in a position to work with you people." He didn't have to add the other half of that—how he'd also be in a position to hurt them if he felt they'd been unfair. It was a cold, deliberate attempt to demonstrate his political power. And it worked. There was no labor endorsement for Hum-

phrey. I spent some time with my old contacts in the
UAW, beating back any effort to put that union—the
biggest one in Wisconsin—on record as supporting
Humphrey.

Working in Wisconsin also taught me about the
Kennedy approach to politics, and maybe to life—a
kind of headlong, full-speed-ahead approach. The first
time I lived through it firsthand I thought it was going
to be my last.

It was in March, 1960, and Kennedy was due in
Milwaukee for a half-hour live appearance on a local
TV station, WTMJ, which was all the way across town
from the airport. As usual, Kennedy was late, and his
plane, the *Caroline*, landed about a half hour before
broadcast time, in the middle of the rush hour. Five of
us jumped in the car: John Kennedy in the front seat,
Ted Kennedy, Kenny O'Donnell, and Ivan Nestingen
(mayor of Madison and a Kennedy supporter) in the
back seat, and me in the driver's seat. As we zoomed
out into traffic, I realized that I didn't know exactly
where the station was.

The next half hour was right out of Keystone Cops.
We came to a red light, and there were twenty cars
backed up.

"Pass 'em," Kennedy yelled.

"There's no room," I said from behind the wheel.

"The other lane," Kennedy said. So I swung into the
oncoming lane, and with my hand on the horn we
got up to the intersection.

"O.K. on the left," Teddy shouted from the back
seat.

"O.K. on the right," John Kennedy yelled, and off we
went.

At one intersection a cop was directing traffic.

"What do I do now?" I said.

"Do what you were doing before," Kennedy said. So
up we went to the intersection.

"O.K. on the left," shouted Teddy.

"O.K. on the right," Jack yelled.

Just as we sped through the red light, the cop turned around. I never saw a look of shock like that on anyone in my life. Oh yes—we got to the television station forty-five seconds before Kennedy was supposed to go on the air.

I know that I got even with Ted Kennedy, though, even if it wasn't intentional. He'd mentioned that he was a skier, so I entered him in a ski jump outside Madison. When he got into the state and asked what his schedule was, I told him about the contest.

"Jump?" he said, and he did—straight up. "I told you I skied. But I've never jumped in my life." I have to admit, though, he went through with it and did pretty well—but he told me to call him before I ever scheduled him in anything again.

The Wisconsin primary turned out to be indecisive. Kennedy won, but the delegates split and a lot of the press said we won because Wisconsin was a heavily Catholic state. In West Virginia, they said, with only about 4 percent Catholic, it would be different.

I sure thought it would be different. We had gotten a kind of system together in advancing trips: Joe Gargan, a Kennedy cousin and an original advance man from Massachusetts campaigns, John Treanor, and I would take different towns and hit them three or four days in advance. The religious thing was unbelievably bitter. In fact, people had to kind of inform us secretly if they liked Kennedy.

One day Gargan and I were in a small town when a lady came over to us. "I'd like to see you alone," she whispered.

We sneaked off somewhere.

"I overheard that you're going to have Kennedy here," she said. "I just want to tell you that I'm for him." It was like she was offering to sell atomic secrets. "I have a tip," she went on. "Don't put up any signs until an hour or two before he comes. Otherwise they'll tear them all down."

Here, too, the facts of political life, the real hostility

to Catholics and the suspicion of a Kennedy, forced us to do things we wouldn't ordinarily have thought of. We hired high-school kids to pass out handbills door-to-door so that no one could keep the news of a Kennedy visit from people. We bought time on the radio to announce when and where Kennedy was coming. And maybe most important, Kennedy himself found he not only had to face the religious issue head on but also prove to West Virginians that he knew what was on their minds; to leap over the religious issue into gut issues.

Kennedy did both these things. He began to ask people if he'd forfeited his right to be President when he was baptized; he began to talk very tough about how nobody had asked his brother his religion when they had him flying dangerous missions, one of which had gotten him killed. He talked openly about his feelings about separation of church and state.

And he also began talking about unemployment and poverty. Until he saw firsthand the way so many people in West Virginia were forced to live, he'd thought of poverty as an abstract issue. Now, going into town after town, trying to rebut the religious issue, he began speaking emotionally about the outrage of children going without milk or protein or anything decent to eat, about not having enough clothes to go to school, about how there were no jobs.

"I'm not satisfied with this. This country can do better." In a way, his own effort to break through religious hostility forced him to get as close as possible to West Virginia. And a lot of his major campaign themes later in the fall were formed in West Virginia.

The hardest part about West Virginia was that all this hostility blocked us from the one thing the Kennedys liked best: participation of as many people as possible. I remember hearing that in 1958, when Kennedy was running for senator again, there was a a long list of volunteers and no work for them. Some-body—Larry O'Brien, I think—put them to work writ-

ing thank-you notes to all the people who signed
Kennedy's nominating petition. It wasn't vital work but
it meant that thousands of people were actively involved in a campaign, and tens of thousands got a
personal note of thanks from a Kennedy worker.

That kind of involvement was always critical to a
Kennedy campaign. It meant that people weren't just
thinking vaguely about a candidate, but that they
were really involved. In Wisconsin, at the urging of
Joe Kennedy, we had hundreds of people distributing
a tabloid newspaper about John Kennedy. It would
have been cheaper—certainly easier—to hire a distribu-
tion company, but by using volunteers, it meant all
these people and their families felt a commitment to
the campaign. They were thinking about it. They
were arguing the case for Kennedy to their friends.
They were certain to vote on primary day, and to get
out their friends.

Bob Kennedy used to make this point over and
over. "Politicians don't do anything but hold meetings
and decide what work should be done," he'd say.
"What we have to do is to get a little work out of a
lot of people, instead of a lot of work out of a few."

This was rough in West Virginia, but we won that
election with an almost 2-1 majority. And that night
we all felt John Kennedy had the nomination locked
up. That night, at the Kanawha Hotel in Charleston,
West Virginia, we had a victory party. It was the only
time we really celebrated during the entire campaign.
We'd expected to win the other primaries; but this
one was tough, and the win was both huge and a real
step to the nomination. Bob Kennedy was there and
was as happy as I ever saw him in his life; he was
singing and celebrating.

Suddenly things quieted down. Hubert Humphrey
had come in to congratulate the winners. He was
finished for 1960, and he knew it. Everyone felt a little
sorry for him, because he meant well and had fought
hard. After he'd congratulated John Kennedy, Bob

tapped me on the shoulder and said, "Jerry, why don't you drive the senator back to his hotel."

We left the ballroom and walked to my car. It was a bad moment for me, because I'd known Humphrey since Wisconsin when I'd been working for Proxmire. He'd once called me "Proxmire's sputnik" at a dinner, and his people had asked me to work for Humphrey in the primary. He took the loss hard, as anyone would. He had tears in his eyes and was saying things he probably didn't mean, like, "Maybe if I'd had you it would have been different." I'm as much an egotist as anyone else, but I knew damn well that wasn't exactly the difference between Kennedy and Humphrey. But it was a sad moment, and it kind of took the edge off the celebration.

After West Virginia, I noticed something interesting happening to me that's probably typical of most people who work in important campaigns. We began to get more people working with us; the advance operation got bigger, and I got to see less and less of John Kennedy.

And I didn't like it.

There's something about working in politics that makes you feel that the closer you are to The Man Running, the more important you are. I've never seen a political aide, no matter how experienced or influential, who didn't feel this. Speech writers, advance men, whatever, they always want to be close to a candidate, to have the room next to him in a hotel, to be "in the room" if an important decision is made, to be listed as part of his "inner circle." It's probably because this is the payoff in politics. If people think you're always with The Man, you find yourself getting phone calls and requests for help, you find people are more cooperative.

It's sort of like the Kremlin pictures on May Day: the people standing closest to the party leaders are thought to be more important. All I know is that on Kennedy's trips, everyone on his staff wanted the room next to his: speech writer, aide, pol, whatever. I felt the same way, and when I started getting separated from him, or never seeing him as I always did in Wisconsin, I'd start to wonder whether he was trying to get rid of me, or whether the staff thought I wasn't doing my job. There are a lot of sick things in politics, but this feeling is one of the sickest. I've had the disease enough to know how bad it can be.

The stuff I'd been doing really didn't get going again until after the convention, where I'd worked as a "locator," keeping lines open between different members of Kennedy's staff. And it was only after the convention, at a meeting of the basic staff with Bob Kennedy, that anyone bothered to give a name to the work I'd been doing since the middle of 1959. At this meeting in Washington, without any warning, Kennedy's brother Bob said: "I'm going to ask Jerry Bruno to say a few words. Jerry's a real advance man; he did a lot of the advance in Wisconsin and West Virginia, and he'll tell you how it's done."

That's how I found out I was an advance man.

I also didn't have anything to say, except to mention all the details we'd found to be important, and to hammer home John Kennedy's message that you could never take anything for granted. There were no details too small to ignore, because any one of them might foul up an entire trip.

It was during the fall campaign of 1960 that we learned a hundred new lessons, and the whole sense of what advance work was all about fell into place. For one thing, the sheer size of the campaign had grown unbelievably. I remember how, in Wisconsin, John Kennedy would wander down a street in a small town early in the morning, looking for hands to shake; how there'd be almost no press, no staff, no organization. Now there were dozens of press people, innumerable local candidates and officials, and an organization the size of a small army to move all over the country in about sixty-five days. There was no time to sit down and plan an operation in detail: just things we saw and mistakes we made and tricks we picked up on the road.

There's one day I remember vividly, because it helped to start a rumor about me and my work that wasn't true—at least, not exactly.

It happened in Detroit the evening before Labor Day. Traditionally, the Democratic nominee starts his campaign for the Presidency in Cadillac Square, at a Labor Day rally, and that's what Kennedy was going to do. He was late arriving at the airport, and a large crowd was waiting. To hold them back, we had to put up a fence, and the only one we could find was a snow fence, a rickety wooden affair built to control snow-drifts, not people.

As soon as the plane landed and Kennedy stepped out of the doorway, the crowd began to push forward. They knocked down the snow fence and swarmed all over Kennedy, cheering and reaching out to shake his hand.

"My God," Kennedy said afterward, "I can't believe that crowd. How did you do it?"

I couldn't believe it either. But it looked so good on film and in the press that from then on we made sure that crowds surged over Kennedy. I'd have two men holding a rope by an airport or along a motorcade; then, at the right time, they'd just drop the rope and the crowd would rush close to Kennedy. Once again, it was one of those things that just happened. But since then I've been credited (or blamed) with tricks like sawing a police-line sawhorse three-fourths through, so it could break at the right moment. It's not true. But it is true that once we saw the impact of a crowd scene, we didn't think twice before making it a standard part of a Kennedy campaign stop.

Because nothing was really set down in any organized way, the 1960 campaign didn't have a highly structured list of rules for advance men. But one thing we did get back to was the idea of participation in-

volving people of a town or city as much as possible
in the planning of a trip.

Take, for an example, a town of about 250,000
people. Normally, a large hall in this kind of town—
say a field house—will hold about 7,500 people. If you
leave it to a handful of political leaders, they might
put an ad in the paper or rely on a mailing to turn out
a crowd. Then you'd find a candidate facing a lot of
empty seats.

But if you break it down, if you have a wide variety
of interest groups trying to get out small numbers of
people they know well, you're likely to have a much
more successful turnout. My list would run something
like this:

Labor: Personally contact 200 shop stew-
ards and union officials, and instruct each
of them to bring 5 workers   1,200

Business: Ask 100 friendly businessmen
and professional people to bring 5 friends
and colleagues   600

Bands: Get two 30-piece bands, and "al-
low" each member to invite his parents and
5 friends   480

Schools: Approach principals, school su-
perintendents, and members of the Board
of Education, and persuade them to dis-
miss school for this historic occasion. If
possible give personal invitations to each
student for himself plus 3 friends or mem-
bers of his family   2,400

Political Workers: Invite ward chairmen
and chairmen of surrounding villages and
towns, and get a promise from each of
them that they'll bring 30 party workers
and citizens   2,480

Patronage Holders: In a town with a
Democratic mayor who's more or less
friendly, get 50 jobholders of some influ-

ence to bring 15 friends and workers (who can be encouraged to come by circulars, letters, and conversation)   800

Senior Citizens: Provide, say, three buses from homes to and from the hall, and you can get about 150 out   150

Hostesses: Give 50 housewives the title of "hostess," and give them the job of inviting 10 people, with calls to be made from their homes (saves money)   550

This means that more than 500 people are actively working to turn out a crowd, and that more than 8,500 people have been personally invited by friends or colleagues *before* you invite the general public (which is always done). In this way, people have a stake in turning out a crowd; it means that if a lot of people never do any work (which always happens) you still have a very good chance to get an overflow crowd.

But crowds aren't the only important part of a trip. The event itself has to go well, otherwise all you have is a large crowd witnessing a badly planned, disappointing rally or speech. Here again, the key is to get a wide variety of people with narrowly drawn, specific responsibilities. Usually, the best way to do this is to appoint committees for every conceivable job.

Press Committee. This group will set up the press area, make sure that Western Union officials know where to go to pick up the newsmen's stories, and provide food and drink for the press (as well as finding people to pay for it). In advance of a candidate's arrival, this committee should keep a steady flow of stories into the local press, such as "The oldest Democrat west of the Mississippi will greet Candidate X on Tuesday . . ."

Band. This committee does nothing but invite as many bands as is feasible to play along the motorcade route or outside the hotel where a spontaneous crowd will welcome the candidate.

Entertainment. Some local talent has to keep the crowd's enthusiasm up, especially if it's possible the candidate will be an hour or two late. There are always enough budding rock bands or folk singers around.

Transportation. Motorcades mean cars, and cars mean that one or two local automobile dealers should be persuaded to donate cars for the trip. The committee must also provide buses for the press.

Arrangements. This group must book the political staff and the press into hotels, and also avoid such complications as putting newsmen in the same wing as the candidate.

Platform. Unlike platform committees at national conventions, this one literally is responsible for building the platform and making sure there are the proper number of chairs on it. Each chair must be labeled, so that VIPs don't scramble for position while the candidate is mounting the platform to the cheers of the crowd.

Sound. Nothing is worse than a candidate speaking into a dead mike. It's awkward, embarrassing, lousy. So this committee must get a reliable sound system, and should have the sense to test it out thoroughly two hours or so before the event, so that any last-minute repairs can be accomplished before the rally, not during it.

Candidate Girls. Model agencies, college cheerleading squads, high-school pep teams should be recruited into a group of cheerleaders, dressed alike, with straw hats or ribbons, to drum up enthusiasm, as the "Kennedy Girls" did in 1960.

Signs. It's not only expensive to print signs; it looks too manipulative. Instead, get high-school and college groups to hold sign parties, with Cokes and pizza as fuel, during which handmade signs can be lettered. The people with the most original signs can be rewarded with a handshake from the candidate.

Volunteers. These people will pass out leaflets advertising the speech at plant gates, shopping centers, and office buildings.

Telephones. Housewives will call every registered Democrat and extend a special invitation to come to the rally.

Follow-up. This committee gets lists of local people who worked, and who should be thanked by letter or telephone.

None of these rules, or any other set of instructions, could prevent slipups; some of them put gray in my hair years before my time. They happened more than ten years ago, but it seems like yesterday. . . .

There was a day in Ohio, in a small town I'd rather not mention, where Kennedy had come to spend the night before a busy day of campaigning. We'd gotten word from Washington to line up some workers for a filmed commercial about underpaid workers and Kennedy's minimum-wage proposals. I stumbled across what I thought was a great idea: all the maids and cleaning women at the hotel were for Kennedy. Why not use them in our film? I was feeling pretty proud of myself—so proud that later that night, downing a few with the manager of the hotel, I mentioned to him our idea about the commercial.

"Where did you find workers who weren't getting paid right?"

"Right here in your hotel," I said proudly.

"What!" he screamed, and went racing off.

I don't think I followed him. I don't really remember much of anything that happened, because the next thing I knew I was being shaken awake by Kenny O'Donnell.

"Bruno, Bruno!" he was yelling, trying to pour coffee down my throat. "What the hell is the candidate supposed to do today? Where's the goddam schedule?"

I vaguely remembered that I was supposed to get up early that morning to wake up Kennedy and brief him about the day; the schedule was in my head and nowhere else. And right now my head was filled mostly with cotton.

"Bruno," O'Donnell was yelling, "the candidate wants to know what the hell he's supposed to do today." (We never call a candidate by his name, always "the candidate." Why, I don't know.)

Somehow I came around and gave O'Donnell the schedule. I later found out that the manager of the hotel knew Mike DiSalle, the governor of Ohio, and he'd raised bloody murder about using his employees to prove how underpaid workers were in America, and we had to call the whole thing off.

"You know," Kennedy said later, "I'm not very happy about what happened last night, but let's forget it. Just don't do it again."

It was also in Ohio that I had the worst case of Grand Clong of the whole campaign (Grand Clong, a term I first heard from Frank Mankiewicz, is a common political disease, occurring when things get hopelessly loused up and you suddenly feel a rush of shit to the heart: that's Grand Clong).

We had set up a motorcade to a high-school football stadium, where Kennedy was to speak at a rally. The cars for the motorcade were left at the gate outside the stadium, and we all went inside to a big reception. For some reason I got a little restless about five minutes before Kennedy's set speech ended, and I went outside to the cars.

Only there weren't any cars.

"It's a nightmare," I said to myself. "It can't be happening." I started running around, but I couldn't find a single car.

Just then I heard Kennedy's voice saying, "I would rather light a candle than curse the darkness," which was the standard last line of his speech, the one he used as a signal to the reporters that they should head for the press bus. I raced back inside and signaled for Kennedy to follow me. With about ten thousand screaming people behind us, we walked up a hill to a small shack near the stadium. I pushed Kennedy inside and closed the door. Then I stood there trying to figure out what to say.

"Jerry," Kennedy said, "what are we doing here? Why aren't we going to the cars?"

"How's the next stop shaping up?" I said to our local advance man. "Got the crowds there?" I was trying to change the subject, you see.

"Jerry," Kennedy said again, "what are we doing here? Why aren't we going to the motorcade?"

Well, what the hell. I could always go back to American Motors.

"Senator, I don't know where the cars are." I said.

"You don't know where they are," Kennedy repeated. I don't think he believed it. "Well, go out and find a car."

I ran outside the shack and I couldn't believe what I saw: a crowd of college kids were driving away from the rally in a Model A Ford. I asked them—or told them, or begged them—to let me use the car for Kennedy, and they were delighted.

I ran back to Kennedy and led him to the car, still jammed with these kids.

He didn't believe it.

"I don't believe it," he said, but he got in.

The only person more surprised than John Kennedy was the cop we approached to find out where the motorcade cars were.

"Listen," I said, leaning out of the car. "I have Senator Kennedy here . . . "

"I've had about enough of you kids," the cop said. "Get out of here." Then he looked inside the car, and when he recovered, he led us to the cars. What had happened was that a local official, trying to help, had moved all the cars to a more convenient location—only he hadn't bothered to tell anyone else about the idea.

It's things like that experience that can teach you what to do; and one rule we did have was to let each other know what had gone wrong and why. From then on, *nobody* changed a stop until he was absolutely sure it had been cleared by the advance man in charge. Or, for example, this rule: do not separate a candidate from a speech writer if the speech writer has the speech. Coming into Cincinnati, Kennedy had been greeted by an enormous crowd in MacArthur Square, which faced the hotel where Kennedy was to make a speech. We battled through the crowd and into Kennedy's suite.

After a few minutes Kennedy came into the living room.

"Where's Ted Sorensen?" he said. We all looked at each other. Nobody knew.

Kennedy went back into his room, but came out a few minutes later.

"Could somebody please find Sorensen?" he said. Nothing. "Does anybody know where he is?" Kennedy asked. "He's got the text of the speech. I haven't seen it yet."

I looked out of the window at the thousands of people still in the square.

"I think he's caught in the crowd," I said to O'Donnell.

"Try to find him," he said.

"You gotta be kidding," I said. "There's thousands of people out there."

"Try," he said.

I took about three steps out of the hotel and realized it was impossible. I went back up, and Kennedy was just about going through the roof.

As a matter of fact, things worked out. About five minutes before Kennedy was supposed to go downstairs to give his speech, Sorenson staggered into the room, having been battered around by the crowd, but with the speech in hand. The next morning a Cincinnati paper noted how important Kennedy's speech was, since he read it word for word to make sure he wasn't going to be misquoted.

As the campaign moved into the last month, I began to understand how important this work was. At times, if I stopped and thought about it (which I didn't do often), it was kind of silly, spending hours and days worrying about the mechanics of a campaign appearance, holding furious debates with local politicians about the shape of a platform or how many dignitaries would be allowed into a motorcade (it got so bad we invented the idea of a "VIP" bus to pack in dozens of important people without making the motorcade eight miles long).

But then I began to see what it meant. To the press it meant that Kennedy was coming on strong, and by October a lot of the big papers and magazines were speculating that Kennedy looked like a winner. He was outdrawing Nixon; his crowds were more enthusiastic. We could feel the enthusiasm on a Kennedy trip, and you could read of the tension and the irritability in the Nixon camp (I've been on losing campaigns, too, and you can no more stop the feeling that you're losing than you can stop a case of plague). We could see politicians, observing how Kennedy was drawing, putting out a little more, working a little harder. Because once they thought Kennedy was a winner, they wanted to get on board to be part of the winning effort.

And it worked on Kennedy too. The crowds got into his blood. If they were there, he'd rise to them, speak more forcefully, plunge into them, and send them away with a sense that they had been part of something important and exciting. If the crowds were small, it was like something was missing. The words were there, but the drama wasn't.

On Election Night I was at Hyannis Port, waiting for the returns. There was really nothing to do, except for a pre-election rally at a Boston armory, and we wanted to celebrate. But here, too, we couldn't. As the election tightened up, it was a case of simply sweating it out. Kennedy won, but we didn't taste the real excitement of victory.

Sometime on the day after the election, we were talking about what was going to happen, and a lot of us were saying things like, "Jack will do this or that." Dave Powers stopped for a minute and said, "You know, we can't keep calling him Jack. He's the President now." It was true. And it was all different from then on.

When a President Meets the People

The difference, first of all, is that there's always a man with a black box. He's the first man planned for when you set up a motorcade or a Presidential trip, the first man included on the Air Force One manifest list.

He's the guy who carries the codes that enable the President to order the use of nuclear weapons.

When a political visit is in the making, and the man with the black box is there, it's obvious that it's different doing advance work for a President.

As complicated as my previous experience with advance work was, nothing compared to advancing a President of the United States. Every detail, every moment of a President's time is planned out; as much as possible, no question is left without an answer. But for all this elaborate planning, there's still a lot of seat-of-the-pants political work. That's one thing being President doesn't change.

The best way to show the mix of planning and Presidential politics is to give a detailed example of a typical Presidential trip: in this case, President Kennedy's visit of May, 1963, to Nashville, Tennessee.

The occasion for the trip was to help celebrate the ninetieth anniversary of Vanderbilt University in Nashville. The politics of the trip was the key setting and timing. The civil rights explosion was about to reach the danger point. Martin Luther King's organizing in

Birmingham, Alabama, and the response—the hoses, the police dogs, Sheriff Bull Connor—were all getting national attention. Kennedy was determined to go South, to speak directly to Southerners about this issue.

Vanderbilt University was a good political choice. The place and the occasion were "high level"—there wouldn't be much chance of a redneck disruption, and the audience would at least listen to Kennedy's speech. Also, Tennessee had two liberal senators who were for the most part supporters of the President, Estes Kefauver and Albert Gore. The problem wasn't the city or the university; for me, it was the physical setting of the celebration, Dudley Field at Vanderbilt, the 33,000-seat football stadium.

Crowds are a funny thing. It's always more impressive to fill a small hall than it is to half fill a huge hall. It looks more impressive, it feels more exciting, to walk into a five-thousand-seat hall that's packed to the rafters than it is to see thirty-thousand people in Yankee Stadium. The press reacts the same way. In the first example, they write about an overflow hall; in the second, they'll write: "Speaking to a half-empty stadium, the candidate . . . " Every time I saw a baseball or football stadium in advance work, I'd get a funny feeling in my stomach. One of the first rules of politics is that you just can't fill places that are built to hold that many people. I don't care if I was advancing the Second Coming, I'd rather hold it in a small hall than an enormous stadium.

This time, though, I O.K.'d the stadium site. It seemed that there was no other really suitable site available, that if we handled it right we could make it clear in advance we weren't even dreaming about filling the entire stadium—and that if we really went at it, we could fill it after all.

The first step in plotting out this trip, as all Presidential trips, was to look over the entire route of the trip, from Andrews Air Force Base to the airport, along

the motorcade to the stadium and back. On any Presidential trip, Air Force One always flies the entire
route in advance. The rule is that the President's plane
never—but never—flies into a strange airport. The pilot
must be familiar with the approaches, the runway,
everything. (In fact, so tight is security that if Air
Force One has to refuel—say, at the Nashville airport
—the fuel storage tank is guarded twenty-four hours a
day before the President's arrival—just in case.)

Next, the Secret Service will check the motorcade
route, looking for any possible areas of danger. Any
overpasses or crosswalks will be sealed off by local
police; government office buildings will be sealed off
and shut down, to make that much less the possibility
of a sniper. (Yes, all of these precautions were taken
during the Dallas trip.) As much as possible, the Secret
Service will check all buildings along the route of a
President's travel; if he's going to be staying at a
hotel in town, the Secret Service will get a list of every
employee and run a check to see if there's any possibility of danger. In addition, they'll seal off the entire
floor where a President is to stay, plus the rooms above
and below the President's.

But while the Secret Service's job is security, my job
is getting out a crowd, making the day a political success. So as soon as we knew the President was going
to Nashville—with the word to me coming, as always,
from Kenny O'Donnell—I began to put together the
mechanics of the trip.

In this case, all the political leaders were friendly:
Senators Gore and Kefauver, Governor Frank Clement,
Mayor Beverly Briley. We also had one of our strong-
est press supporters anywhere in the South in the
Nashville Tennessean. So I also got in touch with Amon
Evans, the publisher, and John Seigenthaler, editor
and a former press aide to Robert Kennedy, about the
kind of schedule we should set up. Each of these officials designated a man as his contact—somebody I
could get in touch with for political judgments that

always come up: who rides where, whom should the President talk to, is there any special local issue that somebody may want to talk to the President about. Mayor Briley, for instance, designated an aide named Bill Davis, who turned out to be the guy who had to do all of the toughest mechanical work, and he was great.

I then went to see Alexander Heard, the chancellor of Vanderbilt. (He was the man Nixon wanted as his "liaison" with the college community in 1969, and then ignored when his recommendations got too uncomfortable.) Heard also designated a contact, George McGraw, who was our man at Vanderbilt from then until the President's speech.

The mechanics of getting out a crowd aren't always subtle. For example, a week before Kennedy's visit, Mayor Briley sent a directive to all department heads in the city of Nashville.

"By this directive," it said, "I urge you, all of your staff and employees of your department who are not on critical active duty elsewhere to join with me in representing Metropolitan Government as host to the President."

He then set out, almost block by block, the route of the motorcade and the ways to get to the stadium. And he ended it:

"Your cooperation and that of all employees of Metropolitan Government is earnestly requested."

Governor Clement sent out the same kind of directive to state government employees. Of course, this is one of the things that can be done when a trip is officially non-political—in this case, a celebration of a university's anniversary. But there's no way to guarantee that anybody will show up. We don't put White House aides in charge of checking out how many local and state workers turn out. In fact, one of the worst mistakes you can make is to assume that local political leaders can "deliver" a crowd. (One of the first trips I'd ever done for Kennedy in Wisconsin involved La

Crosse where, everyone told me, a former congressional candidate had it "all locked up." So I didn't do
anything, and sure enough, we got into town to see a
platform, bunting, a band, and *absolutely nobody*
waiting to hear him speak. Kennedy spent an hour going in and out of shops and never went near that
podium. That was enough to teach me not to believe
anybody on faith.)

Instead, we went back to the lesson we learned in
1960—participation. We got every conceivable group
possible involved in bringing people out to hear
Kennedy.

For the airport rally, Senator Kefauver's aide, Bob
Shine, delegated the Young Democrats to turn out
students and local citizens at the airport. Buses were
hired to bring people, and the Young Dems also held
a series of sign parties. This was another lesson learned
in 1960; printed signs or signs with obvious "official"
thinking don't mean anything. Instead, we had volunteers hold "sign-making" parties, where dozens of
people drew their own signs. Once in a while we'd
make a suggestion, but usually people came up with
much funnier, much more original signs themselves.
Then we'd cart the signs out to the airport and hand
them out there and along a motorcade route.

But the worst problem remained those 33,000 seats
in Dudley Field, and how to fill them. Here, too, what
we wound up doing was to pull in God knows how
many different groups and give them a special role
and a special place.

Mayor Briley gave us another enormous bit of help
by proclaiming May 18 "Metro Day"—celebrating both
the President's visit and the new form of "metro"
government that the Nashville area had adopted. This
meant that Briley could use his power to help crowds
get to the stadium—for instance, in setting up shuttle-
bus service from seven locations around Nashville, encouraging out-of-towners to drive their cars in, park
them around town, and take buses to the stadium.

The Boy Scouts were invited to come to the stadium —in full dress—and a special section was set up for them. The Tennessee Federation of Democratic Women began making telephone calls—each member calling ten or twenty people—and tickets were given to them to pass out to their friends. And then it began to snowball.

Our basic idea was simple: if we simply threw open the stadium to people, we would have a miserable turnout. People might think there'd be no room for them; there was no way for them to know where they should sit, or whether there'd be a security guard barring everyone without a ticket. And they just wouldn't turn out. I can't even remember how many local officials told me, "Of course they'll turn out. It's the President, isn't it?" It might have been interesting just once to see what would have happened if I'd done nothing—except I don't think John Kennedy would have appreciated it.

Instead, we printed up tickets for certain sections and made sure that various groups *knew* there was a place for them. In addition to the Boy Scouts and the Democratic Women, we involved other groups:

· Chancellor Heard invited colleges from surrounding areas and sent out 8,000 tickets to those colleges.
· The Alumni Association sent out invitations to 12,000 alumni and their families, with a letter explaining how a special section was being set aside for them.
· Invitations were sent to 8,000 football season-ticket holders.
· Seven hundred boxes were set up, with tickets coming from political leaders, John Seigenthaler, and officials of Vanderbilt University.
· More than 2,000 tickets were sent out by Mayor Briley, again allocating a special section of the stadium for them; a similar invitation list was filled by Governor Clement; in addition, the instructions to government workers reached 18,000 people.

· Congressman Fulton sent invitations and reserved seat tickets to 3,000 members of his campaign organization, made up of any list we could get our hands on.

· Chancellor Heard sent out invitations to sixty-four schools in the Nashville area, inviting students and their parents to hear Kennedy speak. About 120 buses were sent out on May 18, to pick up students and their parents and bring them to the stadium.

I was the only one who knew what all these people were doing. And I never told one group what the others were doing, because each would then assume others were doing the work. If there was duplication, fine—nobody ever complained about getting three invitations to the same event.

All the invitations emphasized that seats were being held only until 10:30 A.M. The President would speak at 11 A.M., and after 10:30 seats would not be held. That way, we communicated two thoughts: first, there was room for people; second, you'd better get there early.

Next, Seigenthaler began to publicize the visit in his paper. For the last three days before the rally, the *Tennessean* was filled with stories about the program, the dignitaries that would be on the platform, the old lady who was walking from Memphis to hear the speech, and everything else that would get the town excited about Kennedy's visit. (In fairness, it *was* the first visit by a President to Nashville in thirty years, and it wasn't as though there wasn't some real excitement about the trip.) Maybe the most important thing was that all these releases kept mentioning that there were 33,000 seats and that *a crowd of twenty thousand was expected.* So by Saturday, even people with no tickets at all, with no invitation, got the message that there'd be room for them.

I guess the most far-out idea we came up with to make it an exciting day and to get a crowd out was the use of bands. John Kennedy just loved bands; he felt they whipped up a crowd and gave the whole day a kind of flair. Maybe it came out of his Boston pol blood, but if a band wasn't at a stop, he'd keep turning to me between handshakes, murmuring, "Where's the band, Jerry, where's the band?"

Well, that day in Nashville we had bands by the busload . . . literally.

Through Bill Graves, director of music and art at Vanderbilt's education department, every school in the area was asked if they'd like their band to welcome President Kennedy along the motorcade route. Each of them was given a specific street corner to stand on and play. The reward for this effort was—a free ticket to the President's speech in a special section! As a bonus, we gave two tickets to each bandsman for his or her parents. Special buses were waiting at each corner. And as the motorcade passed a corner, the band stopped playing, rushed into the bus, and was sped to the stadium, where the bandsmen piled into the special section, along with their parents. By the day of the speech, forty-one high-school bands were lined up, waiting to blare out a welcome for Kennedy, who finally saw enough bands to make him happy.

I made one final decision to try to get the best possible crowd story out of the visit. Somehow we had to show the press that we weren't expecting anything like a capacity crowd at Dudley Field; to prove that anything more than twenty thousand people would really shock us. The press helped, of course, by down-playing the expected crowd, and every official and planner talked about fifteen to twenty thousand people as a top crowd.

We did something else. Instead of putting the platform in the middle of the field on the fifty-yard line, we had it moved toward one of the sidelines and off the fifty-yard line. That way, nobody, especially no reporter, could really think that we were expecting a full house. We'd laid out the stadium as though we were planning on a half-filled house.

On May 18 it all came together. More than thirty thousand people turned out to hear the President; the press stories wrote heavily about the surprisingly warm reception Kennedy received on his trip South; the route was lined with friendly signs, cheering crowds, and brass bands at almost every corner.

And what difference does all this planning make? Does it prove anything at all? I don't know how to prove that it does, except that it kept reminding me about some facts of political life that a lot of people smarter than I have never learned. You can't just rely on a handful of people to do anything, at least not in politics. We got crowds and friendliness when we made a lot of people aware that it was up to *them* to make the President's visit a success. We did better politically when we didn't listen to the politicians who told us how it was always done in the past. And we always did better when we took nothing for granted, when every detail of every stop was checked.

And the details for a President just don't stop. Every place he goes there's an enormous communications set up. The Signal Corps installs a mobile switchboard which puts the President's party instantly in touch with the White House. Once it's installed, it's guarded tightly, even though the location is secret, so that no one can tamper with the lines. And just in case somebody out for trouble does find the switchboard, there's also an emergency radio contact, so the President could relay orders in that way. In a motorcade there's a car with special radio equipment. If the President flies into an airport, there's a switchboard set up there.

(I can remember in the fall of 1962, President Kennedy was coming to Springfield, Illinois, for the congressional campaigns. As soon as he landed and went to pay a ceremonial visit to Lincoln's tomb, he said, "Get me to the telephone." He was utterly unconcerned about the crowd, about what kind of a day it was going to be, about whether he was going to make

political points. We were, I later figured out, right in
the middle of the Cuban missile crisis preparations,
and he was trying to stay in touch with the latest
possible developments.)

So important is the President's time that I found
myself using every possible device to save it for him.
On trips to other cities, for instance, the biggest payoff
I could give a hard-working volunteer was a chance to
meet the President personally. I could win a friend
for life by just letting someone shake John Kennedy's
hand and hear him say "Thanks."

But I also knew that if I brought a handful of
people into the President's suite, I'd never get them
out. It's natural enough; the effect a President has on
people is hypnotic. It's as if you can just *feel* all that
power and you can't break loose. So, instead, I'd bring
a volunteer into a separate room, and the President
would come in, say hello, give him a word of thanks,
and then be able to leave without any awkwardness.
It's a small, tiny detail, but it's the kind of thing
I spent time worrying about when working for a
President.

In fact, some of the things people do to impress a
President can't be imagined if you haven't seen them
with your own eyes. For instance, here's what happened when President Johnson went to Minneapolis
for a Swedish Day celebration in June of 1964.

In the first place, this was during the mystery about
whom Johnson was going to pick for Vice-President.
Two of the leading contenders, Gene McCarthy and
Hubert Humphrey, were from Minnesota, and aides of
each of them started knocking my door down, explaining how either Humphrey or McCarthy should really
be the one to stand next to Johnson. It was also a
great, harmonious occasion for me, because everybody
thought I was secretly helping Bob Kennedy get the
Vice-Presidential nomination; not that there was an
awful lot I could do as an advance man, you under-

stand, but suspicion in politics is like air—it's all around you all the time.

All the same, jockeying for position is a normal part of a President's trip—I've seen more fights about who gets to sit next to the President than I have over any real issue—but this trip had a special element of insanity. The Swedish Day celebration was going to be held in Minnehaha Park. And as we were walking through the park, one of the festival's officials said, "You know, we're really proud of Minnehaha Falls. They're really beautiful. It would be great if the President could get to see them."

So I started to look around and I didn't see anything.

"What beautiful falls?" I said. "There's no water anywhere."

"Oh, that's right," the guy said. "We've been having a real dry spell this year and the falls are dry. That's too bad."

I suppose it was too bad, but I can't really say I was ripped apart by the idea of not having a waterfall. But I didn't think about how much this must have meant to somebody in Minneapolis. The next thing I know, the mayor has asked the City Council to pay for the money to get the falls going again. The City Council turns it down, the mayor goes to the City Park Board, and they vote to send *fourteen million gallons* of water over the falls on the day Johnson is going to visit Minneapolis—at a cost of $1,400.

The newspapers had a field day with this kind of spending; it got to be a really funny political sideshow, and the flap got back to Washington and I got on the phone.

"Who told you to put that goddamn—who said we wanted you to spend money to get the falls wet again?" I yelled to our contact.

"Well," he said, "it's the President of the United States. We felt we should do it."

And what happened for all of this uproar and for

fourteen million gallons of water? In the middle of Johnson's speech, we got a report that there was a man with a rifle in the area. So the Secret Service rushed Johnson from the platform to the car, *and he missed the goddamn water!*

When the President Goes Abroad:
My Career as an International Diplomat

You might think that all of the chaos and yelling and screaming drifts away when a President travels abroad on a state visit. Not in any way. It's worse. Maybe it sounds better in Spanish or French or Italian, but it's still the same old business of who gets to sit closest to the Big Man, whose ego has to be massaged this minute, and how we can keep as busy as possible not doing much of anything.

And the crowds? That's always the first thing a President—or any other traveling official—will care about: Is he popular abroad? That's why Robert Kennedy was planning to make a quick tour of Europe in 1968: to show that of all the candidates, he was most admired and known and respected abroad. He was the one man who could make America a symbol of something in the world.

And this crowd worry; it's not just with Presidents or with Presidential candidates. Even in late 1970 when Pope Paul went to Asia, the press wrote about "disappointingly small crowds" at the airport, or the enthusiastic greeting along a motorcade.

When John Kennedy visited Europe in the summer of 1963, I was assigned to advance the Naples stop. I'd stopped over in Dublin where Kennedy was going to launch his European visit, and the feeling in Dublin was unreal. People were literally talking about Ken-

nedy's visit in the streets, in a pub where I stopped
for a beer, everywhere. When I mentioned to someone
in the pub that I worked for John Kennedy, the whole
place went into an uproar.

But Naples was my assignment, and after listening
to a briefing at the American Embassy in Rome, I
wished I was doing the Dublin stop. Beause all the
jealousies and conflicts in a town in America were
multiplied by a hundred on a trip abroad. First, the
Secret Service, which is always security conscious, is
doubly so abroad. They don't have the FBI to run
security checks; they don't speak the language; they
have to solve their own conflicts with the security
people of the host country, so they're really up-tight.
I always used to say that the Secret Service thought
it was a perfect day if the President went from Washington to an airport to a hotel and back again without
seeing anyone or being seen by anyone. Overseas, the
Secret Service was simply more worried.

Then there were local sensibilities to worry about.
Everybody in Italy had a position; everybody was
involved in protocol. There was a regional governor
appointed by the President of Italy, and also the local
mayor. And because this was Naples, there was also a
NATO base, which was used as the excuse for Kennedy's visit. And that meant more protocol, this time
with military men, which meant color guards and
dress reviews and all that.

It took me two days to get briefed at the American
Embassy in Rome, after which I was an instant expert
on the party politics of Italy. We then went from
Rome to Naples by helicopter for meetings with the
President of Italy, or at least with his representatives.
I found two immediate trouble spots. First, the mayor
of Naples didn't get along at all with any of the President's people, especially the regional governor, whom
the President appointed. So deep was the dislike that
the Italian government didn't want the local government involved at all. And I knew from my experiences

back in America that if you weren't always in touch with local officials, you were in a lot of trouble when trying to plan for a good turnout.

Second, we had trouble resulting from not doing what Kennedy always said to do: make sure of every detail. The idea was for Kennedy to speak at the NATO base near Naples, then motorcade into the center of town right in the middle of the day—just when crowds are the largest. Right? Wrong. Because in Naples, like most places in Italy, everybody goes home for a long lunch. From noon to about 3 P.M., you couldn't draw a crowd if you were throwing money into the streets.

Once again, as always happens in politics—and this trip was politics—desperation, not planning, forced me to try something different. Without telling anyone in our consulate or in the Italian President's office, I had the United States Information Agency arrange a secret meeting between the mayor of Naples and myself.

It was like something out of an Art Buchwald column. We drove to the mayor's office in a USIA car so no one from the President's office or the embassy would have any way of knowing that I was holding this meeting. Outside the mayor's office were guys with feathered hats, swords, beautiful uniforms—I never saw so many uniforms in my life, between the *carabinieri,* the local police, the mayor's brother-in-law, and everyone else.

After a few minutes, I went in to see the mayor with an interpreter—I could understand Italian, since my parents were immigrants, but I couldn't speak it. And I began trying to feel my way to what kind of tactic I should use in dealing with this mayor. I suppose it was instinct, or maybe it was blood, since my roots were a cable car away in the mountains of southern Italy, but I felt I could open up with the mayor.

"Your Excellency," I said, "I represent the President of the United States, John Kennedy. He has asked me to convey his best wishes to you and to give you the respect of the people of the United States."

The mayor smiled and his face lit up.

"The President wishes to express his hopes that his visit to your city will be warm and friendly. It is his last appearance in Europe, and he hopes to be able *to meet as many people of Naples as possible* in his motorcade through Naples. He wishes to know what you suggest to help him *meet as many people as possible.*"

The mayor was very excited and happy.

"No one has asked me to help," he said, "and I am sorry we have made no preparations. But if your President wishes me to help, I will be glad to."

My mind went back to Vanderbilt University and the idea of pulling crowds by extending a special invitation.

"Your Honor," I said (I probably called him every title except "Your Holiness" before I was through), "I wonder if it would be a good idea for you, in your capacity as host mayor, to invite the mayors of all the surrounding towns to be your guests in welcoming President Kennedy."

"An excellent idea," the mayor said. So I took a deep breath and went on.

"What you could do," I said, "is to invite each town's mayor to come to a different street corner and welcome President Kennedy. Then each mayor could invite his townspeople to come to that same street corner."

He was still listening, so I threw in the final gem.

"You know," I said, "President Kennedy loves bands."

The mayor wasn't quite sure he had heard right.

"He loves bands?" the mayor said.

"Yes," I repeated, "he just loves bands."

"Well," the mayor said happily, "we'll have lots of bands. Maybe the mayors could bring bands from their towns to play at the different corners."

I couldn't believe it. If this mayor ever wanted a job as an advance man in the United States, I'd sign him up in a minute!

"That's just a wonderful idea," I said, and thought to myself, "John Kennedy isn't going to believe this. It's just like a campaign stop."

"How about flags and banners?" I said.

"Fine, fine," the mayor said. He was really getting excited about having the President and was becoming committed to the notion of having the biggest reception in history for anyone.

With that, I thought things were looking good and left to help out on some of the other arrangements. The international sensitivities were really pressing in. For instance, the Naples NATO base was located right on the site where Mussolini used to give harangues to crowds in the streets; the tower he spoke from was still there, and I went up to it just to look around. It was not the kind of color story we wanted the press to play with too much. In another case, it took us two days to arrange the timing of the two Presidents' arrivals. The idea was for Italian President Segni to arrive by car at the NATO base just at noon as Kennedy was arriving by helicopter.

But under no circumstances would it be acceptable if Segni had to wait ten or twenty minutes. Both the Italian officials and the American Embassy people were terribly worried about this business of timing. How did we *know* the helicopter could land on time? What would we do if Kennedy was very late? Could we change direction fast enough so that President Segni would not be kept waiting? And we then had all the other mechanics to grind out: who would sit where, who would take the first step to whom, and all those fascinating details. But my mind was still on the crowd.

Then Pierre Salinger called me from Rome. The crowds all over Europe had been fantastic, and in Berlin they would have given the city to Kennedy if he'd wanted it. But in Rome the streets were deserted.

"The President didn't have very many people come out to see him," Pierre said. "He really wants those people to turn out in Naples."

So back I went to the mayor, who was more geared up for this trip than I was.

"I just wanted to tell you, Mr. Mayor, that the President really appreciates all you're doing for his visit, especially arranging for the mayors and the bands. He's just delighted."

The mayor was beaming.

"I wonder, Your Excellency," I said, "if it would be a good idea to let out school. You know, this may be the only chance the children of Naples will ever have to see their President and our President together here in Naples."

It was a bull's-eye. The mayor motioned an aide over, pointed to me and the interpreter, and said, "Take this all down." So I went through a three-minute course in Letting Out School for a Beloved Public Figure.

Finally I shot the last bolt I had.

"You know, it would really be too bad if the shopkeepers and businessmen all were home when the two Presidents came to Naples. Maybe you could have a special day of welcome when all the stores stayed open in the middle of the day as a kind of honor to President Segni and President Kennedy."

"Excellent, excellent," he said. I could have kissed him. This was the one man of all the bureaucrats and officials I'd dealt with who wasn't completely up-tight about protocol and ceremony. Somehow we'd hit it off, and his instincts and mine were the same. He would have done anything to make Kennedy's visit a success, whatever the protocol problems.

I had to show the mayor how grateful I was. So I reached to my tie and took off my PT-109 tie clasp. I held it out to him.

"I want you to know how much I appreciate everything you've done," I said. "Because of your cooperation I know the President is going to have a warm welcome in Naples. So on behalf of the President of the United States and the people of America, I'd like to present you with this little gift." And I gave him the tie clasp.

He really looked touched and happy. He clapped his hands to bring an aide over and whispered something in his ear. A minute or two later the aide came back with a beautifully bound photo book of Naples.

"On behalf of the people of Naples," said the mayor, "I wish to present this to you and to the President."

All of a sudden I realized what had happened. Somehow this mayor, who was an open, friendly man, figured that *I* was somehow the expert on protocol. If I said, "Let's invite the mayors," he figured, that's what they do in the United States. If I said, "Why don't you let out the schools?" he must have figured, they always let the schools out when the President travels. The big lesson I'd learned in politics back in America was that if you looked like you knew what you were doing, and talked like you knew what you were doing, people thought you knew what you were doing—and sometimes it even worked out that way. Since neither the mayor nor I knew a damn thing about real grown-up protocol, we were both inventing our own version of what was proper and what wasn't. The mayor had decided that the only important thing was how many people came out to greet Kennedy, and we both worked our heads off for that.

A helpful part of this insane bit of international diplomacy was the United States Information Agency. They kept me in touch with more than thirty local mayors who were coming into Naples; they had the Italian and American flags distributed to the crowd; and, most important, they kept me from becoming an international incident by hiding my unofficial advance work from the national Italian government.

With one final check on every one of the people connected with the turnout, I went out to the NATO base outside Naples to wait for Kennedy. Rome had gone, as Pierre Salinger said, "very, very badly," and it was up to us to prove that Italy was in fact enthusiastic about the President, and not leave Europe with an anticlimactic stop after the incredible receptions Kennedy had got in Dublin and Berlin. And it was there at the NATO base, as I spotted the helicopters off in the sky, that I got a feeling I'd never had before. In all the other times I'd done this kind of work, it had always been part of my life. There was no solemnity, no moment when somebody had said to me, "Bruno, you are now a part of the official team of the President of the United States," and I'd just gone along, never thinking much about what I was doing or for whom, except that it beat driving a truck in Kenosha.

But now, standing there with all this military pomp all around me, with flags and bands, waiting to start the welcome in motion, I realized that my folks had been born in those mountains I could turn and look at. And now I was waiting for the President. I got a shiver all through me, for the first and the last time, thinking about where I was and why.

The President's trip through Naples was like nothing you would believe. Maybe it would have been that big even if we had done nothing about it, but that's something you never know. The crowds were unreal. They swarmed all over the motorcade; they yelled; they screamed; they cheered. They wouldn't let Kennedy get more than ten feet at a time before they jumped into the path of the car to cheer him and greet him. Believe me, I didn't need any trick with a rope or fence that suddenly fell to arrange this. It was pure passion. Ironically, the very size and enthusiasm of the crowd kept any pictures of it from being taken.

The Italian government had insisted that the motorcade be two car widths wide, so that each cabinet officer could have his own car, with neither Americans nor Italians ahead of the other.

"It won't work," I kept insisting. "Your police won't be able to handle it. Nobody could. A motorcade that wide won't be able to make it through the crowd."

"Don't tell us how to handle crowds," they answered, probably more diplomatically than that. "We've had kings, queens, the Pope, and we know what we're doing."

You know what happened, of course. I was in the communications car only two cars in front of the President's, and ten minutes into the motorcade I completely lost sight of his car. And so did the press. That was the rub. The photographers on the flatbed truck we usually used were so furious about missing the President that they raised their cameras in protest and refused to take pictures. That was supposed to get somebody anxious enough to blow a whistle or something and break up the crowd for the photographers. Anyway, the Italian photographers—the *paparazzi*— make our photographers look like country gentlemen. The motorcade would have taken about a half hour to get from the base through the central business district of Naples. A good crowd could have stretched the time to an hour. It took more than two hours to cover *one stretch* from the district out to the airport where we were leaving for home.

I never saw President Kennedy happier than after that trip—despite the fact that the Secret Service was bruised, their pants and shirts torn, from trying to get through the crowd.

"Bruno," he said, "those were your countrymen who came out to see me—and those bands! Where did you get the bands?"

My God, I thought. Even in all that he noticed bands.

"They just love you, Mr. President," I said.

"Don't give me that—how did you do it?"

He was just flying. In fact, he invited me on Air

Force One to make the trip home, which was something he never did, and he came up and put an arm around me, saying, "Those crowds were fantastic, just fantastic."

Naturally I took the credit. But somewhere in southern Italy is an ex-mayor of Naples who didn't know enough not to do what I asked him. If any Presidential candidate is looking for an advance man for 1972, I think I know somebody who can help him out. I only wish I'd had this mayor with me in the 1960 campaign. It would have been a lot easier.

Actually, my career in international diplomacy began in Latin America in 1962. O'Donnell told me that President Kennedy was going to make a goodwill tour of Latin America, and I'd be going along to set up the stopover in Bogotá, Colombia.

It was like doing the most difficult, complicated advance imaginable in America, but without any of the advantages of training. It was impossible to pop into a bar or walk around town and get a sense of the place. Because you had no sense of tradition, no ability to strike up conversations, no way of getting into the flow of the city. I was a foreigner, period. On top of that, Latin America was a source of enormous worry to the Secret Service, for good reasons. The last time an important American had gone there—it was Richard Nixon in 1958—his reception wasn't exactly friendly. There was worry all over about demonstrating students, Communists, guerrillas, everything. Kennedy wanted to show that an American President could get a warm welcome in South America. But the Bay of Pigs was still on people's minds, and so was the whole question of Castro. A lot of the students idolized JFK, a lot of the governments were scared stiff of him.

My own problems were worsened by the fact that nobody bothered to tell the Secret Service about me. I'd had very little contact with these men, and while they knew Pierre Salinger and Kenny O'Donnell, who were in charge of the pre-trip survey flight to the Latin

American countries, nobody really knew who the hell I was.

So when I was dropped off in Bogotá, and we all went to a briefing at the Colombian government offices, I was still just kind of trailing along behind Salinger and O'Donnell. Then they flew off to the next stop, while I stayed behind to work out the advance. At 8 A.M. the next morning there was a meeting in our hotel. In I walked, and immediately everybody stopped talking and just sat around. I figured, well, just another bull session, and I left to look around Bogotá, to figure out where a motorcade would do best.

That afternoon there was another meeting. In I walked. Nothing. Dead silence. What the hell is this? I thought, and I left.

By the next morning I was almost ready for it. A meeting. I walked in. Everybody shut up. I was about ready to ask what the joke was when a Secret Service agent turned to me, very coldly.

"Could I ask you just one question?" he said. "What are you doing here?"

"Could I ask what *you're* doing here?" I answered. Wit has never been my strong point.

"I'm the agent in charge of this stop," he says.

"Well, I'm Kenny O'Donnell's representative," I said.

"Whats your name?" he asked.

"Jerry Bruno," I replied, getting the answer right the first time. "What's your name?"

"Stu Stout." The name rang a bell. He was the guy I was supposed to look up. Stout then called the White House and got Jerry Behn, head of the Secret Service detail.

"Gee," Behn said. "I forgot to tell you. Bruno is Kenny's guy. He makes the political decisions."

That ended a day and a half of suspicion, and Stout and I got along. We had to, in a way, to keep ourselves sane for the rest of the advance in Colombia.

There was, for example, the Case of the Spy. For

two days she followed us everywhere we went. If we left the hotel, she'd leave the hotel. If we went to a restaurant, she'd go to a restaurant. After the first day one of the Secret Service agents went up to her.

"Who are you?" he demanded.

"No speak English," she said.

We got so jittery wondering who this woman was—a Mata Hari, a prostitute, some spy for the Communists—that we asked the Bogotá police to check her out.

"Describe her," they said. We did and they laughed.

"She works for *us*," the policeman said. "She's looking out for you."

Or take the Case of the Car. Sensibilities are very important on any advance trip, and in dealing with another government, it's important not to insult somebody with a flippant comment or by implying he doesn't know what he's doing. Since I generally tell most people they don't know what they're doing, this posed a rather serious problem for me.

Our liaison man with Colombia's President was a military officer—they *all* seemed to be military men—and his big key point was that Kennedy had to ride in the official car. The Secret Service never liked the President to ride in anything but the Queen Mary—the big bubble-top car—but diplomatically it was a very difficult thing to settle.

Agent Stout was really upset about that idea, since he'd been with Nixon in Caracas in 1958.

"We'd better have a look at their car," he said, and we drove off to see it in their army arsenal.

We couldn't believe what we saw. It had been built in 1936. It hadn't been used in twenty years, and it was a tank! It was absolutely solid armor plate, with tiny little peephole slits and gun slots. It also had four flat tires and a lot of cobwebs.

"Gee," I said, "this will really look great back home. John Kennedy will really be delighted with his reception in Bogotá."

"Well," Stout said, "I'll be damned if we're going to use this car. We'll cancel the trip first!"

It took us three days, but we finally persuaded the Colombian government that Kennedy really wanted to see the people of Bogotá, and that we'd use their cars for the rest of the motorcade.

The balance of the planning was filled with wonderful diversions, like, for instance, the gunfire outside our hotel at 5 A.M.

"What happened?" we asked some Colombian officials.

"Oh," they said, "one of the students was tearing down the welcoming posters. We shot him."

And there was the fact that Colombia broke off relations with Castro right before Kennedy's visit. That was guaranteed to stir up the Left and maybe provoke demonstrations. In fact, the Secret Service had a plan to evacuate Kennedy in case of real trouble. They had a destroyer anchored in the bay and a helicopter on standby. If a crowd attacked, the plan was to bring the helicopter down right over the motorcade, put a jacket around Kennedy like they use to haul astronauts out of the water, lift him into the helicopter, and then take him out of the city to the destroyer. It would have been a terrible sight, but a lot better than having him hurt by a mob.

The trip worked out O.K., except that Pierre Salinger took ten years off my life. After all that effort, one of the worst things that can happen to an advance man is for the trip to be suddenly called off. It's like a speech writer who works his tail off to find the speech isn't being used. Mostly, I guess, it's ego. If you think you've put together a really good stop, you want the man you're working for to see it and to realize what a good job you've done.

Anyway, we were at the Bogotá airport, waiting for Kennedy's arrival. The President of Colombia is there, the Archbishop, the soldiers, the crowd; we're all waiting. Suddenly an agent came running down the runway, yelling, "Bruno, Air Force One is on the line. They've got to talk to you right away."

Oh God, I thought, they're canceling the trip.

I ran to the White House switchboard and picked up the phone. It was Salinger.

"How's it going, Jerry?" he said.

"Fine, fine, great crowd." Come on, I said to myself, what's up?

"Jerry," Salinger said, "we've got a really big assignment for you. Really important."

"What is it?" I said.

"We've got a lot of Catholic reporters with us, and we've got to find a place where they can go to Mass."

"You bastard," I thought, and damn near fainted.

I guess, though, that my all-time triumph as unofficial diplomat came in 1964, when President Johnson was planning a joint ceremony with Mexico to give back some land along the border that had long been a sore spot in Mexican-American relations. The idea was to have the ceremony start on Stanton Street Bridge, right on the border between the United States and Mexico. I'd gone down to El Paso to sit in on meetings with the State Department and the Mexican government to set up the mechanics of the day.

I'd heard a lot of John Kennedy's offhand comments about the State Department, which weren't always too kind, and I'd run into a lot of red tape in Bogotá and Naples, but this planning session was an eye-opener. When Senator Fulbright later started talking about the "arrogance of power," I knew exactly what he meant.

They started in by worrying a lot about how we were going to keep border security in effect during this celebration of trust and friendship. The State Department rep was really concerned about all these Mexicans (you could almost hear him saying "wetbacks") swarming across the border, bringing in their diseases.

"We just can't open up the border. We have health regulations," he'd say. Great. Here's this guy from the Mexican President's office, being told about how germ-ridden his countrymen were. You could see him getting angry.

Then our State Department people started explaining about how *our* government would handle all the details, that the Mexican government didn't have to worry, that we knew how limited their resources were.

Finally they hit the last straw.

"We'll supply all the cars and the gas," State said, "because we know what a poor country you are."

The Mexican representative stood up, furious.

"We may be a poor country," he shouted, "but we are a proud country too." And out he stormed.

Here again, if I'd followed protocol, I would have sat there and done nothing. But for me, the trip was the goal. You couldn't let it go down the drain because of some stupid mistake. So Wilson McCarthy, another advance man, and I got up and ran after him.

"Listen," we said. "Don't listen to those guys. We're from the White House. Let's talk this over."

"There's nothing to talk over," he said.

We then reverted to universal language.

"Let's go have a drink," we said.

So we walked across the border into Mexico, into a small, hot town, and found a run-down bar. We started to talk and drink, mostly drink. At 3 A.M. we were so relaxed that nobody could feel anything. But the entire schedule had been locked up. We called Bill Moyers the next morning, gave him the run-down, and that was how a bright page in Mexican-U.S. history was accomplished.

After watching our foreign policy for the last several years, I'm not sure we didn't hit on the answer to all future arguments between countries. Just imagine if the Paris Peace Talks started with a dozen rounds of good, stiff drinks. We could probably end the war in a week.

Dallas

I was the advance man for John Kennedy's trip to Dallas.

I don't guess there's a day when I don't think about it, keep seeing the route of the motorcade, the route we planned, the stop at the Trade Mart he never reached, the dinner that night in Austin that was supposed to end the trip. I know that for more than a year I blamed myself for his murder. I don't think that way anymore, or if I do, I don't know it. And I don't blame any politician or pressure group for setting up the chain that ended on Elm Street outside that School Book Depository. I don't have any conspiracy theory to offer. But I somehow think it's important to show how all of the tiny, stupid, petty political fights and feuds can shape a complete change in the world, in history. It doesn't prove anything except how dumb it is to think any of us really can control events, how much it's all up for grabs.

The trip to Texas was political from the word go. There was nobody pretending this was a "non-political" tour of oil wells or cactus or anything else. John Kennedy was going to Texas because he had to have Texas to win reelection in 1964, and because Texas looked like a big trouble spot for his reelection.

"It's a real mess," Kenny O'Donnell said to me at the White House in early October. It was only a few

days after Kennedy had returned from his Western
conservation tour, where he'd found the peace theme
that he wanted to use in his reelection campaign: taking on Goldwaterism head-on, speaking about stopping the spread of nuclear weapons and radiation. But
even before that Western trip was over, the White
House was announcing that Kennedy would go to
Texas.

Why? First, Kennedy was in danger of losing all of
the Southern states in 1964—particularly if Goldwater
was the Republican candidate, which everyone took
for granted at that time (it was only after Dallas that
Goldwater became anything except an odds-on favor-
ite). He'd won Texas in 1960 by less than 25,000 votes,
mostly because a bunch of right-wing nuts had spit on
Lyndon and Lady Bird Johnson in a hotel in Dallas
just before Election Day. If there was one Confederate
state Kennedy had to have, it was Texas, with its
twenty-five electoral votes. And his civil rights stands,
with his backing of the law to let Negroes eat anywhere with whites, was making him very unpopular
all over the South, including Texas.

Second, the Texas Democrats were completely, hopelessly split. Briefly, Texas liberals and conservatives in
the Democratic party were so angry at each other that
they were out for each other's blood, first and last. If
we couldn't get the whole party working for Kennedy
in 1964, the state was as good as lost. And that meant
other problems: a lot of the conservatives in Texas
hadn't really been for Kennedy. For a lot of them
Goldwater would be a really attractive candidate. It
was important to do two things: first, to prove Kennedy's popularity so that conservative Democrats
would think twice before they went off the reserva-
tion; and second, to smooth over the split as much as
possible.

Like Kenny said, it was a real mess.

"You'll have to talk to Jenkins," Kenny said. He
meant Walter Jenkins, who was Vice-President John-

son's administrative assistant. "Walter is a pretty good guy, and he'll brief you on the politics of the trip. After you speak to him, check back here and see what sort of thing we can put together."

Jenkins gave me a straight run-down. It was like listening to somebody talking all about an incurable disease. What we had was a governor, John Connally, who was the leader of the conservative Texas Democrats: oil money, corporate leaders, some rural "redneck" strength. On the other side was Senator Ralph Yarborough, a Southern liberal, supported by labor (which was liberal in Texas), blacks, Latin Americans, and intellectuals.

They hated each other. Yarborough had helped to lead a primary fight in 1962 which almost beat Connally. (The liberal candidate was Don Yarborough— no relation to Ralph, but it just shows how confused everything was.) In 1964 both Connally and Ralph Yarborough were up for reelection, and each of them was threatening to lead a primary fight against the other guy. (In 1970, Connally helped defeat Yarborough in the Democratic primary. Later that year he was named by Nixon to be Secretary of the Treasury.) In the middle of all this was Johnson, who was with the conservative big-money wing, but who was also going to be on the ticket with Kennedy next time around and had to play it like a man in the middle.

Somehow the trip had to show that President Kennedy could appeal to both sides, that he had the people with him, and that the conservative and liberal wings of the party had to stand together to help reelect him.

I wasn't any happier when I went to see Senator Yarborough toward the end of October. Yarborough, a maverick liberal in Texas politics, was a supporter of Kennedy, and I liked him. But he was angry and bitter. He described how Connally and Johnson were screwing him; worse, he said, they'd be after John Kennedy in a minute if they thought they could get away with it politically. He was sure that Connally would want to run the whole Texas trip to embarrass him, and as it turned out, he was pretty nearly right.

This was really going to be a wonderful trip; not only would I have all the usual garbage, but every stop, every appearance would be fought over by contacts from the Connally-Johnson wing, versus the Yarborough wing of the party. Right after I spoke with the senator I called O'Donnell at the White House.

"Listen, Kenny," I said, "I know you always give me the best jobs, the easiest trips, and this is really going to top it off."

"Look," he said "it's not the easiest trip in the world, but it's one thing the President wants to do and we're going to have to make the best of it."

With those cheery words I left for Texas.

Just to show how smooth it all was, I'd arranged to meet with Connally's people that night and with Yarborough's people the next morning. But, somehow, Yarborough's people heard when I was coming down, and when I got to the airport, *both* factions were there to meet me. Right away I got into a fight over whom I'd meet with first. By the time I got that straightened out, I was ready to go home and forget the whole thing.

Well, the next morning it got worse. First I saw people from the State Democratic Committee—solid Connally people—and the proposed schedule they showed me was as if all of Yarborough's supporters had moved to Alaska.

There were meetings with nobody but the Connally wing. If there was a black spokesman, it was Connally's house black. The same with labor. The same with Latin Americans. And when I said something about that, I got a really heartening answer.

"You're coming into Texas," the spokesman said, "and Connally is the governor."

"Yes," I said, "but there's somebody above even the

governor, and that's the President of the United States."

As soon as I left the Democratic State Committee, I met with some of Yarborough's people. I have to admit that I was mostly on their side. They didn't want control of Kennedy's visit, just a piece of the action. They were supporters of Kennedy all the way; they were for his civil rights and foreign policy stands, while most of the state Democrats were against Kennedy on the big issues. I think it must have been that meeting, and my sense that I didn't like what the Connally people were going to do, that put my back up for the meeting I then had with Governor Connally.

It was a really friendly atmosphere. Connally was at the head of a long conference table. He's a tall, handsome guy, and he was wearing cowboy boots. He really looked the part. All around him on either side of the table were his aides. And I was sitting there, by myself, bootless, about eight feet shorter than he was. At one point they brought in lunch: a juicy steak for Connally, a sandwich for me. And I'll tell you, if you've spent most of your life working with your hands, you know what they're trying to tell you with a move like that.

As we sat there, Connally began outlining the schedule for Kennedy's trip. It was firm, he kept insisting; it was his state, and if the President didn't like it, he could stay home. That really made me feel good.

"I just want to tell you one thing, Governor," I said. "He's the President. I'm here to get everybody's recommendations, and I'll forward them to the White House. But they'll decide."

With that, Connally jumped up from the table, grabbed a phone, and said, "Get me the White House." Then we all waited. "Get me Kenny O'Donnell." Then he started talking about the entire schedule: here's what's going to happen in Houston, here's what we'll do in San Antonio. Then we wait.

"Fine, fine, I'll get back to you," Connally said. And

he came back to the table and started in, saying, "This is what we want him to do."

I learned only later—a lot later, when it really didn't make any difference—that Kenny had told him the same thing I had, that it was the White House that would make any final decision.

Anyway, we went around one or two more times, and then Connally just got up and left.

"You know," Cliff Carter said to me, "you really handled that all wrong."

Despite all of this fighting, the trip began to click into place. Kennedy would start in San Antonio, then go to Houston, then to Forth Worth, then to Dallas for a luncheon, then to Austin for a big fund-raising dinner, and home to Washington. The one impossible spot on the whole trip was Dallas.

We knew Kennedy would go someplace for a luncheon speech. The question was where. The original plan was to go to the Hilton Hotel, but the group that had booked the hotel ballroom wouldn't give it up. That brought the possible locations down to two: the Trade Mart and the Women's Building auditorium at the state fairgrounds.

The location for a speech shouldn't really stir anyone's emotions, but in fact it was really a matter of deciding what kind of trip Kennedy would make and whom he would be allowed to speak to.

The Women's Building was a sprawling auditorium which could hold four thousand. To fill it, we would probably have opened the place up after lunch was served so the people in Dallas could have come in and heard Kennedy. We would have organized labor committes, chicano committees, women and blacks, to turn people out. It would have been a way for Kennedy to say symbolically, "I want to speak to all the people of Dallas."

The Trade Mart was an enclosed setting. The lunch would be an expensive affair, but more important, it would be closed off. It would have been totally under

the control of the Dallas Citizens' Council—no relation
to the White Citizens' Council, but the establishment
group that ran that town's politics, social life, and
everything else. A Trade Mart luncheon would be a
rich people's luncheon: a way of identifying Kennedy
with the Dallas establishment.

There was one other key factor in the choice. The
Women's Building auditorium was a low-roofed affair. That meant the luncheon dais could only be one
level high—so that everybody was sitting on the same
basis. At the Trade Mart you could build tiers on the
dais. And that's what Connally wanted to do, so that
his allies could sit with the President, while Yarborough was put as far away from Kennedy as possible, to
prove who had clout and who was out of it—the Rus-
sian May Day idea again, that the closer you were
to Number One, the more important you were.

There was another point about the Women's Building site that didn't seem important to anyone at the
time. If Kennedy had been going there instead of to
the Trade Mart, he would have been traveling two
blocks farther away from the School Book Depository
—and at a much faster rate of speed. At that speed and
distance, it would have been almost impossible for a
sniper to hit him from the Depository.

With the Dallas site the only unresolved part of the
trip, I got back to Washington on November 5 and
reported back to O'Donnell. There were still problems
—Yarborough said that the Connally-Johnson operation
was sitting on its hands, not doing anything to help
sell tickets to the Austin fund-raiser on Friday night,
November 22. It occurred to me that this could be a
funny kind of political move. If Kennedy appeared
weak on this trip, it could have bolstered Connally's
bargaining position in 1964 by telling Kennedy:
"You're in trouble in Texas, and you need us to win.
Don't try anything funny, like helping to fight Connally for governor next time around."

But it was the Dallas luncheon problem that was

on my mind, and I decided to use the Secret Service ploy. I'd always been a kind of natural opponent of the Service, since their goal was security and mine was pulling out crowds. If thousands of people stopped a motorcade to greet the President, that was a triumph for me. The same occasion meant trouble—big trouble —for the Secret Service. But still, their word on security was final. They could by law order a President not to go some place, on security grounds, and he was bound to obey them.

My idea—and I'd done it before on political advance—was to get the Secret Service to veto the Trade Mart on security grounds. That way there was nothing Connally could do about it, and we would have to go to the Women's Building. I asked Jerry Behn, the head of Secret Service at the White House, to pass the word to the Texas agents to wrap it up. But somehow or other that word never got through. We heard back from Texas that the Secret Service had O.K.'d the Trade Mart as acceptable from a security point of view.

So until less than a week before Kennedy's Texas trip, the Dallas luncheon site was the one part of the trip that hadn't been locked up. It's for this reason that I was never able to believe the conspiracy stories afterward. The motorcade routes for every other city were released weeks in advance. Anybody planning to kill the President could have planned it for any city *except* Dallas—because the motorcade route wasn't known until a day or two before the President's visit.

On November 18, the advance men for each city were sent to Texas. In planning for this trip, and in testing our ideas for 1964, we decided to try a new approach. I'd stay back in Washington, at the Democratic National Committee where I worked, and local men would go into each stop. That way I could check every detail by phone without having to run around. I'd still go into cities in advance to look them over, but my time and energy could be spent in working out last-minute problems, from a central desk where an advance man could reach me.

On that same day, Kenny O'Donnell called me from the White House.

"We're going to let Dallas go, Jerry," he said. "We're going to let Connally have the Trade Mart site."

It struck me at the time that this was one of the few fights like this I had lost. I was no inner counselor to John Kennedy or anything like that, but usually, if I fought hard enough, I could generally get my way about what sites he would do best at politically. On things like this my judgment was usually taken. This time it wasn't. I suppose in the end the White House decided that Connally had too much power to screw them in Texas, and that they had to keep Connally happy enough so he wouldn't bolt or sit on his hands for the 1964 election. Because Texas was too vital to lose. Also, it was a case, I think, of the squeaky wheel getting the grease. Yarborough's allies were solidly for Kennedy. There was no chance they'd bolt in 1964, no matter how ticked off they were. With Connally and his friends, you just couldn't be sure.

On the night of November 20, Kennedy flew to Texas. At a time like this an advance man really gets tense. Is the weather going to hold? Will the people bring signs? Will the crowd be friendly? What about hecklers? Will the advance man get the key to open the President's suite, or will he have to stand in the hall for twenty minutes? Will the press get their typewriters and baggage? Will we lose the motorcade route? And suddenly he's on the way, and if it breaks right, it's like the curtain going up on a hit. The bands play, the crowd cheers, the speech gets applauded, and the President is in bed, the day's gone well, and we got through it.

From the time Kennedy landed in San Antonio, it looked like a great trip. The crowds were enormous at the airport, friendly all the way into town. We just had one problem: Senator Yarborough wouldn't ride with Vice-President Johnson. He was so ticked off at the treatment he'd gotten, he wouldn't do it. The press was noticing it, and I relayed word to Houston to the advance man: "Make damn sure Yarborough rides with Johnson."

In Houston, Kennedy had another great stop. I'd told the advance man to forget the schedule and take Kennedy and Jackie to a Latin-American dinner for a drop-in appearance. It was terrific, with Jackie saying hello to them in Spanish. But in Houston, Yarborough still wouldn't ride with the Vice-President. So I got back on the phone, this time to Fort Worth, where the President would spend Thursday. "Yarborough and Johnson have got to ride in the same car," I said.

Friday morning the party left Fort Worth for Dallas. Since it was only thirty miles away, we'd debated whether to fly there or motorcade the entire distance. In the end, we decided to fly because the motorcade would take Kennedy right by the General Dynamics plant, where the TFX airplane was being built. There was a lot of flak about that plane—its cost and where the contract had gone—and we thought it better if Kennedy had nothing to do with that place. So instead Air Force One flew the short hop to Dallas. And finally, with Kennedy himself making the pitch, Yarborough had agreed to ride with Johnson.

Sometime after 1 P.M. Washington time I checked in with Dallas. I was trying to reach Jack Puterbaugh, our Dallas advance man, to find out how the crowd looked in this city where Adlai Stevenson had been almost physically attacked a few weeks earlier. I raised the Secret Service agent through the White House switchboard and asked for Puterbaugh.

"How's it going?" I asked.

"We got off good at the airport," he said, "and the motorcade looks good."

"Can I get Puterbaugh?" I said.

"I'm not sure where he is right now—let me raise the motorcade and I'll get back—"

All of a sudden he stopped.

"I got to get off, I got to get off," he said, and his voice sounded different. "There's trouble with the motorcade, trouble in the motorcade, I got to get off."

And I was cut off.

There were a dozen things I was imagining: a blown tire, a friendly crowd stopping the motorcade, a wrong turn, a right-wing nut that had run out to spit on the President—everything except what happened.

I called back the White House switchboard and asked for Dallas.

"There's been some trouble down there," the operator said. "We can't get through."

Just then a secretary came running up.

"Jerry, Jerry," she was yelling. "The ticker's got a light flashing. They say the President was shot."

I ran over to the Associated Press wire, with a red light flashing, meaning urgent story coming, and there was the flash: PRESIDENT SHOT.

I tried the White House switchboard. The operator was crying.

"We can't get through," she said, sobbing. "The President's been shot."

And it all came back to me. All the police chiefs and Secret Service warnings that always seemed so stupid; all the worry and the jokes about assassinations; all the preparations I'd always laughed at.

Then I was angry, furious, at Connally and his demands to control the trip, where Kennedy should go, and now the President had been shot because we went here instead of there.

And then I thought about me—about how this was the one time I didn't just stick up and fight like a son of a bitch for the place I wanted to go. I never realized how my decisions could be this important. I'm involved with the murder of a President. And then, for the first time in my life, I started to cry.

I left the National Committee and went over to the White House. I guess I stayed there all night, and it was never real, none of it: the floodlights, the announcers, the body being brought back to the White House—it was all like a bad dream. I wandered around, watched Sarge Shriver beginning to plan the funeral, and I did nothing.

I remember only two things about the next few days. The first was the funeral, where I sat with one of the big women newspaper writers. All through the Mass she was crying, and as we left she grabbed me.

"Jerry," she said, "you've all got to stick together. You can't let Lyndon Johnson run the country."

I thought of that a lot in the next few years, because she became one of Johnson's closest buddies and used to rip up Bob Kennedy all the time.

The other thing I remember is that when they were taking the casket down Pennsylvania Avenue on Sunday, I was standing in the crowd. Somebody had a transistor radio and a bulletin came over that Oswald had just been shot. And a woman standing there put her hand over her face and said, "My God, when is this all going to end?"

In some ways, it never did.

Epilogue

I spent a few weeks with the Committee, sending out Mass cards and notes to people who'd worked really hard for John Kennedy, and wondering what I was going to do. I'd just assumed Kennedy would be President for eight years, and then I'd figure out my life.

But there's one memory that tells you something about Washington and the way it is down there. A lot of times I would go to Duke Zeibert's for a beer. And sometimes Kenny O'Donnell would come in. Whenever he'd enter, the place would come alive.

"Kenny O'Donnell's here," you could hear them say,

because he was Kennedy's appointments secretary and a political insider. People would run over, buy him a drink, say hi. It would make their week; they could tell all their friends. "You know who I had a drink with last night? Kenny O'Donnell!"

About three weeks after Dallas, we met at Duke's for a drink. Kenny O'Donnell came in, and nobody moved. Not one guy said hello and offered to buy him a drink. It was all Jack Valenti or Bill Moyers. They had clout now. They were the dear old friends. People Kenny had gotten jobs for would kind of ignore him. And the same people who three years ago said, "Thank God we got new blood, what a fine guy Kennedy is," now were saying out loud, "Johnson really knows Washington. He'll be great." If I called somebody in government, the same people who'd drop everything to take my call wouldn't call back at all. Because I was a Kennedy man, I was out of it.

Washington is so cold and cruel you can't explain it. I'm glad it happened in a way, because it taught me. I wouldn't be fooled that it was my brilliant mind or thoughtful ideas anybody liked. In fact, a few weeks later, Moyers asked me to set up a trip. And within twenty-four hours the word was out. I was in again, I was O.K. My calls were returned, my old friends were old friends again, because I was in with LBJ.

Really inspiring.

Lyndon Johnson

I didn't like Lyndon Johnson.

I suppose part of it was unfair. I was in politics mostly because of John Kennedy, and Johnson was the big opposition in 1960, even though he wasn't in any primaries. There was some bad feeling you just can't get rid of in politics. After John Kennedy's death, a lot of us felt Johnson was President because of what had happened to Kennedy in Johnson's home state. Then in 1965 I went to work for Bob Kennedy, and Johnson was the big political opponent there, especially after Vietnam.

But that isn't entirely it. After you take all the personal feelings into account, I think it comes down to the fact that, as somebody once told Johnson when he asked how come people didn't like him, he really wasn't very likable.

He never gave me one of those famous tongue-lashings or threatened my job or anything like that. In my case it comes down to watching politicians with people. I just had this sense that Johnson wanted people to love him, but that he couldn't really relate to people, he couldn't watch people's faces and react in an open situation, and that he'd almost try to push people into caring about him.

There's a story that's told about Hitler (no, I'm *not* making that comparison) that maybe points this up. Hitler was reviewing the troops one day, and somewhere in the ranks a man sneezed.

"Who sneezed?" Hitler says. No answer.

"Who sneezed?" Hitler shouts. Nothing. So he orders the whole front row of troops mowed down with a machine gun.

"Now who sneezed?" Hitler says.

And from way back comes this voice, "I did, *Mein Führer.*"

"Oh," says Hitler. *"Gesundheit."*

There's something about that in Lyndon Johnson.

I didn't see Johnson at all until 1960. It was right after the election, when Kennedy went down to Johnson's ranch in Texas to pay a visit. All during that day Johnson kept saying, "I was the leader and Jack Kennedy was a soldier. But now Kennedy's the leader and I'm the soldier. I just want to help him." He said it over and over, like he was trying to convince himself.

I remember, during that visit, Johnson got really mad because the Secret Service was installing a White House phone for Kennedy.

"Doesn't he trust me?" Johnson kept demanding. "We won't listen in." He couldn't believe that this was standard White House procedure, that Kennedy's people weren't trying to snub him. I remember also that he decked out Pierre Salinger in a Western outfit. He looked so ridiculous I almost fell over laughing. In fact, Johnson even tried to put a Western outfit on John Kennedy, but Kennedy politely refused. And maybe the high point—or low point—of that trip was the one night Johnson brought me into a meeting, *introducing* me to Kennedy. He looked at me like I was nuts, being introduced to my own boss by a man I'd never met before.

I also watched Johnson a little bit when I was at the President's Committee on Equal Employment Opportunity, which was a job I did from 1961 until 1962. It was a kind of base from which I could do advance work. Johnson as Vice-President was the chairman, and he and his people—George Reedy, I remember, who later was White House press secretary—would always try to juggle figures to prove they were doing the job of getting blacks a chance at jobs. If no blacks were working in high-paying jobs, they'd take all the job categories and add them up, to make the performance look good.

Bob Kennedy as Attorney General came to a lot of meetings and saw through it. He'd always ask, "How many blacks have jobs that pay more than seventy-five hundred dollars a year?" and questions like that which would really get under Johnson's skin. They never did like each other, and that series of meetings on equal employment was one of the big reasons.

But I never did any advance work for Johnson until after he became President. In early 1964 Johnson wanted to take a swing through parts of Appalachia to dramatize his War on Poverty, and also to come back through Pittsburgh. Already there was talk of backlash, and the White House wanted to bolster Johnson's strength in a real white labor town. Pittsburgh, of course, was the steel center, and his relations with the United Steel Workers were very good.

I remember that we really worked hard on that trip to prove that we were trying to do our best. Kenny still was at the White House, and since Goldwater might be Johnson's opponent, we sort of told ourselves that Kennedy would want us to help beat Goldwater, and he had picked Johnson, after all. So we turned out really good crowds in Rocky Mount, North Carolina, and in Pittsburgh.

After the trip, I went back to the White House to tell Kenny how well I thought the trip had gone, and Johnson walked into Kenny's office.

"Did we really get a big turnout in Pittsburgh?" he asked. "Did you really try?"

Kenny looked completely disgusted.

"We did our best," he said flatly.

I just couldn't believe it. If anything, we had bent over backward to prove we weren't making Johnson look bad. I don't think it was cruelty. It was just a kind of indifference. John Kennedy never got bubbly, he never really went out of his way to say something, but somehow or other he made us know he appreciated the work we were doing. We never felt any of that from Johnson.

It was on this same trip, at Rocky Mount, North Carolina, that I saw another quirk of Johnson's. He was speaking to a large crowd outdoors, through a portable speaker's stand. The horns were put very far away from him to let the crowd hear what was going on. But *he* couldn't hear himself, and I guess he didn't realize that everybody else could.

So in the middle of his speech, he turned to Jack Valenti and said, "Turn that sound up." And Valenti just went berserk. He started running all over to find the controls.

"They're right next to you," I said.

"Turn it up, turn it up," Valenti said. "They can't hear the President."

I ran to the technican, and he said, no, the volume's on full, it's just that Johnson can't hear himself. That's what I told Valenti.

Meanwhile, LBJ stopped speaking and turned to Valenti again. "I told you to turn that sound up. Now, dammit, do it."

Valenti knew there was nothing wrong, but there was no way to tell Johnson. And he just turned white.

It was a farce. Johnson was standing there, shaking the mike, saying, "Get this thing going." Valenti was shouting at me, "Jerry, do something, do something." I was yelling back at Valenti. "For Christ's sake, Jack, there's nothing you can do."

I learned that lesson: from then on, we put a built-in speaker right under the speaker's stand so that Johnson could hear himself. But it shook me up. That kind of hysteria just wasn't the way John Kennedy had taught me to work.

Another thing I couldn't swallow was the hokey things Johnson liked to do. Maybe it was snobbery, but

John Kennedy couldn't abide corn. He'd never put on a hat or kiss a baby. It just wasn't him. When he waved to a crowd, he did it with a half-gesture, a kind of flick of the wrist. Johnson was just the reverse. He made you feel he wanted to swallow everyone up.

In 1964 a bad tornado had swept through Indiana. There was death and an incredible amount of damage. The White House decided on the spur of the moment that LBJ should take a swing into the worst areas.

Now, it's my job to look for angles. I'm not trying to say I was a sentimentalist. In fact, on this trip I had a sheriff take me through Elkhart, and he showed me a place where a family had been wiped out.

"Haven't you got anything worse?" I asked.

So I could pull things like that. But when Johnson got there, he started visiting a wrecked home, and then he spotted a heap of demolished house trailers. He headed right for them. I couldn't understand what was happening, until I saw that at the very top of the heap was an American flag. LBJ scrambled to the site, climbed up the heap, and just stood there, head bowed, while the photographers started snapping like mad.

The whole rest of the trip, the press was razzing me. "Bruno," they said, "how could you be that corny, putting that flag up there. Boy, how gimmicky can you get?" There was no way I could convince them that this was all Johnson.

The most disturbing thing I saw, although it didn't register at the time, was that in most places Johnson couldn't hold a crowd. He could *attract* a crowd for a lot of reasons. He was President, he'd done a good job after Kennedy's death in pulling people together, he was popular at the time, and he was the hope against Goldwater. But he had no sense of how to speak. After about fifteen minutes, people would start drifting away. I saw him literally empty a hall on more than one occasion.

I wonder if that inability to look at people and relate to them was part of what brought Johnson down in 1968. I always thought that if he'd been able to feel more accurately, he never would have had all those "credibility gap" stories. By 1967, no matter how people felt about Vietnam, they didn't like Johnson because they didn't trust him; he couldn't arouse them or appeal to them. But maybe if he'd been a better listener, he wouldn't have made such a big thing of Vietnam.

Anyway, I couldn't get rid of this feeling that I just wasn't in tune with Johnson or the people around him. At the 1964 Convention, for example (that's where they designed a fireworks display that ended with a picture of Johnson in the sky), his staff, particularly Marvin Watson, almost drove me crazy. They sent memos that everyone had to be at work by 9 A.M., no more than a half hour for lunch—the kind of rules that never work in politics and just cause bad feelings.

The one that topped it for me, though, was a memo from Watson warning that girls couldn't wear half-slips.

"No half-slips?" some secretary would say. "Why no half-slips?"

"Well," I'd say, "official policy," or something dumb like that. And then I'd go ask somebody, "What is this with half-slips? Is this a joke?"

But the clincher with Watson came during the fall campaign—and again, it was a glimpse into what got to Johnson. Hecklers are a part of any campaign; something that politicians just live with. Sometimes they help—as Richard Nixon found out. In 1970 his advance men always let just enough hecklers in to shout, but not enough to disrupt. Then he could denounce them before a cheering audience.

John Kennedy always used to notice them. If there were twenty-five thousand people cheering for him, he'd see the one nasty sign.

"Did you see that bastard with that 'go home' sign?"

he'd say. "What has he got against me? What do you suppose I did to him?"

And Bob Kennedy used to kid with them, to play off them. Once, in 1968, Kennedy spoke in Omaha at a rally. One very loud heckler kept interrupting him, shouting at him. Finally Kennedy turned to one side.

"Ethel," he said, talking sadly to his wife, "I have some bad news for you. The vote in Omaha is *not* going to be unanimous."

But Johnson couldn't stand them. Early in the fall campaign, Marvin Watson, who was overseeing the advance work, said that the President was very angry at the hecklers.

"The President does not want them," Watson said. "See if you can eliminate them."

At the very next stop, one man had an enormous "Goldwater for President" sign that Johnson just couldn't miss. And sure enough, there was Watson.

"I thought I told you we don't want any more signs and hecklers," he said. "Now get that down."

"It's impossible," I said. "We sent some people over there, but you can't tear down signs. It'll just look really bad."

That, I thought, was the end of it. But as I was getting ready to leave, Watson called with a great idea. What about itching powder? he asked.

Itching powder?

Sure, Watson said. Our advance men could carry a can with us. If they saw a heckler shouting or carrying a Goldwater sign, the advance man could throw some powder on the heckler, who'd have to stop what he was doing.

Well, I never did get around to using it, although in Houston, I heard, somebody did use it on some unfriendly people. I just kept visualizing the White House after Vietnam; and how maybe somebody had tried to convince Dean Rusk to take some itching powder with him to the Senate Foreign Relations Committee.

Some Great Battles I Have Fought

There's nothing really rewarding about being denounced in front of five-thousand people by a congressman, or having a near fistfight because of where somebody sits in a motorcade. It's just one of those things—or two or five of those things—that I ran into in politics. It just seemed that, working for Robert Kennedy, I happened to run into them all the time.

For a lot of reasons—some of them because of his brother's murder, some of them because of the extraordinary kind of man he was—people were drawn to him. He drew the wildest, most enthusiastic crowds I ever saw. Although we had worked hard to get crowds out, we had nothing to do with the kind of response I saw.

In 1968 we put Robert Kennedy through the most unfriendly territory imaginable—or so we thought. We sent him through southern Indiana, which is practically in the Confederacy; we sent him through Hammond and East Chicago, where the backlash was born. And when people came to see him, to listen to him, it worked. They went away liking the guy or trusting him. And I know as sure as anything, if we hadn't had that personal campaign, if we had tried to run Robert Kennedy just on television, it wouldn't have been the same. He needed to see people and talk to them face-to-face, and they needed to see him. Fifteen minutes on a whistle-stop, watching Kennedy ask the kids in the crowd playful questions, watching him trying to answer people's questions even at rallies, and the ruthless thing just faded, went out the window. I've never seen anything like it before and probably won't again.

But one of the problems with this attraction is that every politician, everybody who wanted glory or attention, wanted to be around Robert Kennedy. We were just about overwhelmed by the number of people who wanted to go along on campaign swings, not because they had anything to do, but because they wanted to be around Bob Kennedy.

Sometimes it even inflicted staff people. In 1967, Kennedy went into upstate New York to visit a migrant work camp, where people were living in incredibly wretched conditions. One of the people who went along was a girl from the Washington office, whom I'll call Betty. She was tall and very shapely. As the group went into the camp, Kennedy got into a near-violent argument with the camp manager, who had a gun. It was a tense moment, and when we finally got in, it was clear that his visit would have a real impact on people if he could be seen with families living in buses with the seats ripped out and made into excuses for homes.

But Betty couldn't move more than four feet from Bob Kennedy. It wasn't that she was trying to hog attention or get into pictures, it was the magnet working. But it simply wouldn't make any impact at all if, instead of having Kennedy with these children and families, all the press got was pictures of Kennedy and this tall, good-looking girl. So I kind of walked near her and smiled sadly and said out of a corner of my mouth, "Betty, get away from the senator."

Nothing. She just wouldn't move. So I tried again. "Betty," I said a little more grim now, "get away from the senator. Let him alone." She still wouldn't move.

Finally I'd had it. "Betty," I said, "either you get

away from the senator or I'll drag you by the hair into that car."

With that she ran off in tears. The next day I got a call from Joe Dolan, Kennedy's administrative assistant, who wanted to know how I had pulled it off.

"Pulled what off?" I asked.

"That great story about the girl from the Kennedy staff who was so upset at what the conditions were that she broke down and cried."

See, there *is* a God.

I wish all of my efforts to set things up had gone as well. There was one time in 1966 when Kennedy was going into California to help out Governor Pat Brown and his ticket. One of the people on that ticket used to work with Bob Kennedy in Washington and had gotten the senator to promise to help. It turned out that he wanted Kennedy to spend two hours in the middle of the day at a fund-raising cocktail party. And Kennedy was not about to confine himself to seventy-five people when he could be seeing seventy-five thousand in that same amount of time. So we had to cancel that.

The local candidate was livid. He called the office where, as usual, I was made the heavy. That was always the deal; it was never Bob Kennedy's cruel decision, but mine. You know: "Gosh, that's too bad, but you know that Bruno, vicious to the teeth."

Well, we decided we could make it up to this candidate by getting him into the motorcade in Bob Kennedy's car. It was a long motorcade, lasting several hours with lots of stops for speeches and rallies, and after the first stop it was clear the whole thing would be a disaster. This candidate couldn't keep still; he'd jump up and wave hysterically and climb over Kennedy to turn and wave in back, blocking Kennedy from the people.

After the first stop, Kennedy said, "For God's sake, get him out of here." And after the second stop, this

guy raced over to the car, screaming, "Wait, wait!"
and jumped in, and the whole mess began again.

Finally, Kennedy reached the breaking point in
Sacramento, where this scene had repeated itself. As
the rally broke up and the candidates headed back to
their cars, I simply slammed the door in this guy's
face, pushed him away, and said reasonably, "Get the
hell out of here."

This guy—he lost, by the way—went into a literal
rage. People really do turn purple, I found out then.
I thought he was either going to fall over dead or
kill me. He was kind of gurgling, so angry he couldn't
get any words out. And then he did get some words
out, like:

"I'm not going to take this! I won't be insulted like
this! I'm going to get you!"

I called a cop over and asked for help.

"Get this guy in a car and look out for him." And
as the motorcade pulled out, I remember two things:
first, the smile on Bob Kennedy's face, and second, this
voice off in the distance, screaming, "Bruno, Bruno,
I'll get you . . ."

That dispute, however, was nothing compared to my
fight that same year with Congresswoman Edith Green
of Oregon. This whole swing was being done for a
couple of reasons: to help Democratic candidates for
Congress and governorships, and to win some points
for Kennedy. Just in case anything happened in 1968,
it would be a good idea to have looked into a lot of key
states; and as a primary state in Presidential years,
Oregon was very important. But after what we went
through, I'm not sure it was worth it.

Edith Green is a very tough politician—one of the
toughest anywhere—and as a lot of badly scarred
people in Washington will tell you, when she wants
something she knows how to fight for it. She's also
somebody Robert Kennedy felt a debt to, because of
her help to John Kennedy in 1960.

Now my business was crowds: how to get them out,

where to get them out, even how to count them. (It was a ritual in any campaign stop. The newsmen would yell, "Bruno, what's the crowd?"

"Fifty thousand," I'd say.

"No way, Bruno. Twenty thousand," they'd yell back. So we'd settle on forty thousand.)

Edith Green had her ideas about what Bob Kennedy should do—namely, speak at this new auditorium in Portland that seated 14,000. Remember the first rule of crowds: 25,000 people in a 50,000-seat stadium is a half-empty turnout. But 4,000 people in a hall that seats 3,000 is an overflow crowd. And it works that way on a crowd. People want the sense of being somewhere special, somewhere a lot of people are trying to get to. It depresses people to see empty seats all around them, makes them feel they've been conned into turning out for an event that wasn't all that special.

In this case I took a look around and realized that you couldn't fill those fourteen thousand seats if Raquel Welch and Paul Newman put on a stag show as a warm-up.

So I called the Washington office.

"Joe," I said to Dolan (he let me call him by his first name after about a year), "you just can't fill this hall Edith wants us to go to. It'll just be terrible."

"Well," Dolan said, "don't do it."

So I looked around and found a Labor Temple that was perfect. It held maybe four thousand people and I knew we could get an overflow crowd out to that auditorium. It was just right. At least, that's what I thought until I spoke to Edith Green.

"That Temple can't hold the crowd that's going to turn out for Kennedy," she said.

"How many do you think will come out?" I asked.

"Maybe six thousand people," she said.

"Yeah, but that won't even half fill the new hall," I said. "It'll be terrible."

"Why can't we hang a curtain over the empty seats?" she said.

This is a common trick in political advance, and it really works great in places like the old Madison Square Garden where you can barely see the balcony from the floor. The press never notices those things. But when we went out to look at this new hall, it was one of those well-lit modern places, with no posts and no hidden corners. There was just no way to hide eight thousand empty seats, not from newsmen, and God knows not from Robert Kennedy.

The argument showed no signs of settlement, so I settled it myself. I had thousands of flyers printed up announcing that Robert Kennedy and Edith Green would appear at the Labor Temple. Edith Green just about hit the ceiling and threatened to cancel the whole affair.

"I don't think you can do that," I said. "You've got fifty thousand flyers saying you and Kennedy will be there. That could mean a lot of disappointed voters."

So Bob Kennedy came to Portland, and at the Labor Temple they were hanging from the rafters, and I mean literally up there in the rafters. There were two thousand people or so outside, the hall was packed, the press was impressed by the turnout, and it was the kind of evening Kennedy loved. And then Edith Green stood up to introduce Kennedy.

"I want all you people to know," she said, turning in my direction, "that had I had my way, we would all have been comfortable and been able to hear Bob Kennedy. But because of that man there"—and she points to me—"we're in this crowded, sweaty room. And I want you to know, Senator Kennedy, that it was that man who caused this problem."

There I am—my first public recognition in all my years in politics! And there's Bob Kennedy, his head down as though in deep thought, trying to keep from bursting out laughing on the stage.

The upshot of this squabble, by the way, was that

in 1968, when Kennedy announced for President, Edith Green agreed to head up his campaign in Oregon subject to a few conditions—one of which was that I would not be allowed to come into Oregon at all. So I didn't. And that was the one primary state we lost. Naturally, I'm not suggesting Kennedy lost Oregon because I wasn't there. Of course not. Of course.

I think maybe the most embarrassing scrap I ever got into was a result of a common practice in Washington and politics: namely, promising more than you mean to do. I guess the Kennedy campaign promised the Vice-Presidency in 1960—or implied a promise—to enough people to field a baseball team. LBJ held out the same promise, so did Nixon, and so will any other candidate. And those kinds of promises are made all the way down the line.

If you blow into town and some girl spends twenty hours a day knocking her block off to help turn out a crowd, you're likely to say to her, "You know, if we win this thing there's a job for you in Washington." For most people, it's payoff enough—they'd really be a little frightened to leave their hometown, but they can always tell themselves, "If I'd wanted to, I could have worked in Washington—maybe the White House."

But sometimes people take it seriously. My own thought usually is that if somebody really wants the job I promised him or her enough to come to Washington to bug me for it, when they've proved they're hard workers and I'll find a job. (One guy from West Virginia borrowed $20, took a bus to D.C., and spent three nights sleeping on a park bench before he found me. I got him a job. Hell, anybody with that much drive can't miss.)

But one guy in an Ohio town was too much. He'd really helped bring together warring factions of the Democratic party, and at one point I'd said to him, "You know, if you can get this thing together and if Kennedy gets it, you just call and I'll help you out."

Well, the guy called me and asked for help in getting a federal judgeship. In the first place, I wasn't exactly King Kong in Washington. I had a job and I did political work, but federal judgeships are important posts. Also, Robert Kennedy was Attorney General, and the one thing he made really clear was that they had enough politics without anybody mucking around for them. In other words, I could no more get this guy a judgeship than I could get him the Vice-Presidency.

As it turned out, he did get the judgeship, but through no help of mine.

Then came 1964, and I was back in Ohio for Lyndon Johnson. I made the mistake of calling Judge Brown (a clever phony name).

"You know," he said, "you weren't very helpful to me. I needed a favor, and you promised and didn't do it."

Well, O.K., sometimes you bluff.

"What do you mean?" I said. "You got the judgeship, didn't you?"

This is one of the helpful things about politics—nobody really knows who did what to—or for—whom.

"Well," he said, "maybe you're right."

"Of course I'm right," I said. "You'd never have your goddamn judgeship without my help."

"O.K., maybe I've been unfair. But this time I really need help."

It turned out this judge wanted a job for his brother, as far away from Ohio as possible. The brother had been throwing the judge's influence around in order to engage in some very shaky kinds of business. The perfect solution, the judge figured, was a Washington job. Maybe he thought they were all crooks there and it wouldn't be noticed. I promised the judge help, but this brother couldn't have gotten clearance to clean the steps of the Capitol.

Right after the election, the judge called me.

"What about that job, Jerry?" he asked.

"Well, we're working on it, but it's kind of tough,"

I said. And as the calls kept coming from Ohio, I just kept ducking them until they stopped entirely.

Then came 1968, and back I go to Ohio for Bob Kennedy. I pick up the phone and call old Judge Brown for some delegate help in this big non-primary state.

"Hi, Judge," I said. "It's Jerry Bruno."

"You bastard," he answered, "you son of a bitch."

Well, anyway, he remembered me.

"Not once—twice, you conned me, twice! You never did a damn thing for that judgeship and you never got that job for my brother!"

"You know," I said, changing the subject, "Bob Kennedy's going all the way, and if you'd help out with any delegates, then—"

"Bruno," the judge said, "I've had it up to my ears with you and I don't give a shit what you tell me. Get lost."

Which just goes to show you can't win 'em all.

Robert Kennedy: The Last Advance

This is mostly about what happened after Robert Kennedy was murdered. It's going to be very hard to understand some of the things that went on: how people who devoted years of their lives to Kennedy could simply throw themselves into planning his funeral, almost forgetting that there was a good man dead; how people could laugh and tell stories on the plane bringing Robert Kennedy back to New York for the last time. You have to think of an Irish wake to understand it—to understand how the intense work that went into planning Bob Kennedy's funeral was the only way most of us could pay any real tribute to him.

Everyone who worked for Robert Kennedy had the shadow of assassination around him. At least two people on his 1968 campaign said flatly he would not live the effort out, and during his 1968 campaign one network told its camera crews to be around Kennedy at all times, just in case somebody tried to kill him. Kennedy's Senate offices—in Washington, New York City, and the one I ran in Syracuse—regularly got letters from people threatening him.

We had some taste of this in 1966, when Kennedy went out campaigning for candidates for the House, the Senate, and for governor in various states. Out in California, the state police had received a report from a hitchhiker, who'd been picked up by a white, male American, forty years old with a beard. This driver had shown the hitchhiker a mail-order catalogue with a rifle offered. He'd said, "You see that rifle? I'm going to buy that rifle and kill one of the Kennedys."

Well, we were out in California, going from Berkeley to Oakland for a fund-raising party for Congressman Jeffrey Cohelan. The senator's car was overcrowded—it always was, since every local politician and office-seeker wanted to ride with Bob Kennedy—so I jumped out and ran back to the second car with Joe Dolan, Kennedy's administrative assistant, and Jim Tolan, one of his best advance men. We were driving along when a car passed by on our left, with three oddly dressed men. One of them was a white, male American, about forty, with a beard. They pulled abreast of the senator's car, and it suddenly dawned on all three of us that this could be real trouble.

Dolan yelled, "Jerry, Jerry, the beard!" and I jumped out, ran ahead—the motorcade was moving slowly enough—and leaped in Kennedy's car, wedging myself between the senator and the other car. Kennedy looked at me like I was crazy. I'd just left his car to cut the number in the front seat to three, and now I'm coming right back in. He didn't say anything, but he gave me that look: the cold, blue eyes, the look that said, "Something funny's going on here, and you guys don't want me to know about it."

Dolan and Tolan swung around behind the senator's car and cut off the stranger's car when it tried to pull abreast of the senator again. Tolan and Dolan jumped out and raced over to the car. The three guys jumped out—they couldn't figure what was going on. Tolan walked over, grabbed the keys out of the car, tossed them into the bushes, and snapped, "What do you guys think you're doing?" I have a feeling they might like to ask us the same thing.

That was it: we simply went back in our cars and drove off. It seems like odd behavior, maybe; but if you add up the coincidences and the behavior of that strange car, it was enough for us to take some action. What must have happened was simple enough: three guys spotted Robert Kennedy and wanted to have a look at him. From their point of view, we were bullies; from ours, they were a real threat.

That same trip drew some other bad times. In Great Falls, Montana, an FBI agent went up to Kennedy to tell him they'd received a threat that "Kennedy dies at four." We were due to speak in Butte, Montana, at 4 P.M., outside in a setting surrounded by tall buildings. It would be an ideal spot for a man with a gun. Kennedy sent the agent to talk to Dolan and me. We were, of course, thrilled that this guy had told Kennedy he might have five hours to live, and Dolan spent quite some time asking what the hell this FBI guy thought he was doing that was helpful by telling Kennedy that information.

"Well," he said, "those were my instructions."

Dolan filled me in on the problem. I reacted immediately.

"Joe," I said, "you've gotta stand behind him every minute."

"Why me, Jerry?" says Dolan.

"You're taller," I said. We grinned at each other and that eased the tension a little, but we still had to decide what to do. We couldn't cancel the appearance or anything, but we did decide to use a closed car. And that's what we did—in spite of Robert Kennedy. There was no way to kid him that this was some ordinary decision: the skies were sunny, cloudless, a perfect day for motorcading in a convertible. When we got to Butte, we arranged it so the only open car was the press car, and Dolan rushed over to Stan Tretick, from *Look*, Bill Eppridge from *Life* and Steve Shapiro —all three great friends. Dolan says to them, "Listen, you guys stay inside this car, and no matter what happens, don't get out. Stay in this car." They knew from Joe's voice that something serious was going on and they just nodded. The point, of course, was to make sure Kennedy didn't get in that convertible.

Then Robert Kennedy comes over to the closed car. "Joe, Jerry, where's the convertible?"

Senator Metcalf is there; Paul Cannon, who was running for governor, is there, and everybody's kind of looking at everyone else.

"Let's go," Joe says. "You ready, Senator?"

Kennedy glares at us. Hard.

"Joe, the convertible?"

Dolan: "Senator, get in, please."

RFK: "Joe, the convertible?"

Dolan: "Senator, get in."

Kennedy climbs in with Cannon and Metcalf, and we all ride for three blocks, very quietly. Kennedy finally looks up and says, in a very, very cold tone, "This isn't related to the other, is it?"

Senator Metcalf says, "The other what?" And Dolan, who can look like a choirboy when he has to, says, "What other, Senator?"

And Kennedy just looks up, absolutely furious, but saying nothing. It was another false alarm, although we did spot a man in a suit with a rifle across the street. We told the sheriff, who went totally berserk, blasted out over his walkie-talkie, and came back sweating buckets and said, "It's my man."

This went on a few more times. Once in Wyoming, in the face of a threat, we decided to take Kennedy out the back door. He always preferred to move through crowds. He finished the speech—we were in Casper, Wyoming—and he said, "Jerry, let's go through the crowd."

"Fine, Senator," I said, knowing damn well there was a car waiting for us at the back exit. We get off the platform, and I said, "To the left," and Kennedy just automatically responded. By then, we're out the back door and into the car.

It was at this point that Kennedy let us have it. We drove to the hotel, with everything very, very quiet, and he said to us, "Would you come to my room with me?"

We got there—Dolan, myself, and Adam Walinsky, the senator's speech writer who was helping us surround the senator. And for forty-five minutes Kennedy talked with us.

He looked around—to Adam, to Joe Dolan, to me—and he said, "You three have managed to figure out a way to get me from one place where there's five thousand people to another place where there's five thousand people without me seeing any of them. I want it to stop. If someone wants to kill me, they're going to kill me. I do not want to live from day to day with this constant threat. I want to make it clear to you, I want it to stop right now."

It wasn't so much anger, I think, as it was Kennedy's way of telling us that he understood his life was always in danger, but that he couldn't live his life in fear; that there was always a way for someone to kill him if they wanted to badly enough. He often said that "those who write don't shoot and those who shoot, don't write." It was like he had spent his days since Dallas trying to live without that cloud around him, and we were bringing the cloud around him just by trying to keep him safe. Anyway, after that experience we constantly had to find new devices, like breaking up the line of cars at the airport, so the senator's car could get away fast if there was a threat. It got to the point when he was running for President that bomb scares, like in Salt Lake City, Utah, or threats of snipers, like in Lansing, Michigan, just after Reverend King was killed, were sort of expected. And when I would go into a town to feel people out about the race, you'd hear people say, "I like Kennedy, but they won't let him live to be President."

As it turned out, maybe Kennedy had a better sense than any of us of what he should do. Because, on the night of June fourth in Los Angeles, he was shot not while going through a crowd as he liked to do, but

while avoiding a crowd by taking a shortcut through
the kitchen of the Ambassador Hotel. It's the sort of
thing you think about over and over; if I'd been there,
he might have insisted on going through the crowd
after his victory speech to the reception for the press
in the press room. I remember that we had had a
reception on the Sunday before the primary, and Bob's
cousin, Polly Fitzgerald, had asked us to take him
through the kitchen because the crowds would have
been impossible. I said to him then: "Senator, do me
a favor and go through the kitchen because Polly asked
me and I promised her I'd do it." Kennedy just grinned
and said, "I'll do it."

So that Tuesday night the kitchen route was familiar
to everyone. After he got through his speech, he saw
a hand in the crowd guiding him—he always looked
for a familiar face and would follow—and one of the
hotel officials was there, waving to him, and they went
through the kitchen, where Sirhan was waiting. . . .
Would it have been different? How the hell can you
say? It's something you just keep thinking about. . . .

I wasn't in California then. Joe Dolan was getting
reports about New York, where the delegate primaries
would be held on June 18, and the reports weren't
good. The regulars who were officially committed to
Kennedy were sitting on their hands, some of them
actually for Humphrey, and McCarthy was very strong
in Manhattan, and Kennedy really had to do well—it
was the last chance to show primary strength, and it
was his own state. So Dolan asked me repeatedly, with
good reason, to get back to New York and start things
moving.

It's odd, thinking back on it, because this was one
election night I wanted to stay around. Usually I'm
trying to set up the next week's stops, and I really get
turned off by the hangers-on who come out of the
woodwork for the big party—you know, the people
who've never worked a day, and they come for the
feeling of being in the room and part of the festivities.

But this was the big primary, and I felt an urge to stay.

I saw Dolan during the day—it was a dull day, with reporters and campaign aides playing touch football and just waiting in limbo for the returns, and killing time—and he called me sometime in the evening and asked. "How come you didn't leave yet?"

I said, "Joe, I got a flight at ten-thirty—but I'd really like to stay. I never stayed for an election night, and I'd really like to stay for this one."

Dolan insisted. You should understand, by the way, that shouting was a normal conversational tone with us.

"Jerry," Joe said, "for Christ's sake, get on that goddamn plane. You can't do anything here, and we got that big campaign in New York and it's all coming apart. We've got to get it going."

He was right, of course, but I turned to one of the secretaries and said, "Get me a different flight, say two or three A.M. If I don't hear from you, I'll be on the ten-thirty." I later found out she'd got me a later plane but couldn't find me. And you see, that's when your mind really runs away from you, because you start asking yourself, "If I'd only heard from her, I'd have been with Kennedy, and maybe we would have avoided the kitchen and it all wouldn't have happened." It's a good way to go crazy.

I got on the plane from L.A. to Cleveland, on my way to Niagara Falls, New York, where the senator's upstate swing would begin. We were planning a massive two-week blitz of New York, along with an effort to knit up some of the wounds, and to really go after the big money-big labor Johnson-Humphrey alliance. I was asleep when the stewardess shook me awake about 1 A.M.

"Are you Jerry Bruno?" she asked. I said I was.

"The pilot would like to see you," she said. I went up to the cockpit with her, half asleep, not knowing what in hell was going on, whether it was some practical joke or something.

I went into the cockpit and the pilot looked at me.

"Are you Jerry Bruno?"

"Yeah," I said.

"Are you a member of Bob Kennedy's staff?" the pilot asked.

"Yes, I am."

"Sit down," he said. I did, and he turned to me.

"He was shot."

"What did you say?" I said.

"He was shot. He's not dead, but he's very critical."

I just sat there. I didn't believe it.

"We'll let you know if we hear anything," he said, and I just went back to my seat.

I got off at Cleveland, and American Airlines sent somebody to put me on the first plane back to L.A. I'll never know who did it all, but they had a police car and we went right to the hospital.

All during that flight back I was in a kind of shock, thinking about all the threats, thinking about all the times after Dallas when people would talk about Bob and say, "He's gonna get shot," thinking about why I wasn't there, still thinking about the trip upstate, the swing through hostile country where Bob had pulled so well in 1964, and how we could do better now.

I got to the hospital, and I could tell right away he was going to die. Steve Smith was there, Pierre Salinger, Ed Guthman, Dave Hackett, Andy Williams, Jimmy Breslin, and the family. Steve got me aside and said, "We want you to stay here."

There really wasn't anything to do at first but wait for the surgery to be over, and then they gave him a very, very slim chance to pull through; about a half hour later they came back and said he's had it, it's only a matter of time. About 3 A.M. Steve Smith said, "Let's start making arrangements." And everyone knew what he meant.

Now it's at this point that an explanation is necessary—because to an outsider, with Robert Kennedy still alive, it might seem callous to start thinking about his funeral and to start getting on telephones and planning for this event. But that's the only thing that made any sense. We could grieve and cry, but Kennedy always used to say when something went wrong, "Don't tell me what I should have done, tell me what to do now." And that's why we did what we did. We knew there was no hope, we knew there was no way we could cure him, or save his life, and all we had left was to give him the kind of tribute he deserved.

It was Steve Smith who directed the entire operation, almost like a quarterback giving each man a specific job to do. I called Jim Tolan and told him to get a hearse and start figuring out what airport we would land at. We started talking about the Mass, how it ought to be at St. Patrick's. The train was not in anyone's mind just then, but we talked about who would ride in what cars and the plans for burial. And when I'd look up, it would hit me, "Jesus, Robert Kennedy's going to die," but there was no time for grief, and in a way that was good. You function like a machine, you want to be ready and do it right. Weird, I know, but nobody there was any different, not those who worked with the Kennedys.

Ted Kennedy and Steve went in to see Bob, and when they came out Steve asked, very calmly, how things were going. It would sound so cool, so calculating, if you didn't know these people, the whole life-style of doing something and moving on to the next stage. We were doing that thing again, and it seemed natural. Once in a while Andy Williams, one of Bob's best friends, would go out for sandwiches and coffee, everybody looking for something to do. I went out once or twice to talk to some of the press, those that had been his friends, but never mentioned anything about the funeral. And the press—they were no different from any of the crowd—they forgot about getting the story. They were asking how Bob was, was he going to make it.

It was about 8 P.M. on Wednesday night—the night

of June fifth—that the Kennedy family raised the possibility of a train. Kennedy loved the whistle-stops we
had done; he felt they had really brought him closer
to the people than airport stops, and they made for a
warmer kind of campaigning. Once the idea of a train
to take Bob to Washington had been raised, it seemed
like the right thing to do. We called John Ellis back in
New York. Ellis was a college student who was a
natural political worker, and he'd put together most
of the whistle-stops, and we told him to start moving.

I guess it was 11:30 at night when Ted asked me,
"Do you want to go in? It's only a matter of time now."
I went in and saw him with Ethel leaning next to him,
holding his hand, and I watched the breathing bag,
barely moving. I just stood there and looked at him;
with all the medical stuff it wasn't really him, and I
left. I didn't want to go in again and see him, so I
lay down and went to sleep. That's when Pierre
Salinger came over to me and said, "He's dead."

There was no pause—we continued working on the
arrangements for his funeral. It was almost as if we
knew the rally was going to take place, and we had
been waiting for a decision as to whether Bob was
going to show up. It's sad to even talk about it like
that, but that was exactly the sense of the planning
there at Good Samaritan Hospital. There was nothing
else to be done.

In politics egos always clash and disputes erupt
about everything connected with a campaign—who
gets to ride with the candidate, who gets to introduce
him, who gets invited to his hotel room Election Night.
Well, the first thing that had to do with Bob Kennedy
after he died was one of those incidents.

To understand it, you have to remember the mayor
of Los Angeles was (and is) Sam Yorty—a man who
has had a bitter feud with the Kennedys, beginning
with Jack. A Democrat, he backed Richard Nixon in
1960 (mostly for religious reasons), and he and Bob
Kennedy got into a furious fight at a Senate hearing in

1966. He beat a black candidate for mayor in 1969—by using every racist and fear-mongering trick in the book. Anyway, every time Bob Kennedy came to Los Angeles in 1968, there was some hassle. At one point, having always refused to provide police escorts for motorcades (which a city will do for any candidate for President), Yorty had his cops ticket every car in the motorcade. It was a mean-spirited, bitter kind of fight.

So we finally wound up hiring a private, paid escort, who worked very well, and whose guys seemed to like Kennedy a lot. Well, the morning of June 6, which was the day he died, we brought the casket downstairs to the hospital lobby, and I went out and lined up the motorcycle escort. All of a sudden an L.A. policeman came over to me.

"What are they doing?" he said, pointing to the escort.

"They're gonna escort the body," I said.

"Oh, no, *we* are," the cop said.

I started to blow up; you know, cool and calm as everybody seems, there are some very close cases when a man I cared this much about has been stupidly killed; I was in no mood to listen to the pettiness that seems to flourish in some people.

"Oh, no," I said to the cop. "You didn't when he was alive, you're not going to escort him when he's dead."

So this cop—a sergeant—went and got a lieutenant, and we went through the same drill.

"I'm running this show," the lieutenant said.

"The hell you are. You had a chance to protect this guy and you didn't want to protect him. He doesn't need protection now, he's dead. What are you going to protect now?"

He walked away, and a minute later our escort came up to me.

"Jerry," he said, "we've been told that if we get within a block of that body, they're going to take their motorcycles and run us into the ground. We just don't want to cause a problem. We loved the guy, it's an honor, but we don't want to get into a fight now."

So we used the L.A. police—I know there were a lot more angry words, and our escort lined up a block behind the hearse and drove out with us. If this all sounds stupid and petty, maybe it is. I can't explain how people react when this kind of shock hits them, or what difference it would make to Bob Kennedy—but there's a feeling that it was important to carry through on what was crucial when Kennedy was alive. Maybe when we got angry at this kind of fight, it kept us from going off the edge with sadness.

We got to the highway, and there were crowds along the streets leading up there. Funny, but people were a lot sadder in a way than for John Kennedy, sadder openly, I mean. Maybe it was because John Kennedy was President and they stood in a kind of awe at the Presidency, but with Bobby it was a guy whom they liked, who wasn't surrounded by pomp, whom you could be more emotional about.

When we got to the airport—it was the West Imperial Terminal at L.A. International, the one they use for charter flights—there were five thousand people there. And I had to laugh a little inside, because it was always the hardest place in the world to get a crowd out. No matter what we tried, we could never get more than five or six hundred people, and here there were ten times that many to say good-by.

We boarded that plane—it was Steve Smith who decided who would fly with the senator back to New York, and take my word for it, if you don't think there was social climbing and egos involved about who was or wasn't on that plane, you're wrong—and it was like an airborne wake. People were recalling stories about the campaign, and about Jack's campaign, and about some of the crazy experiences in the race. There was laughter, and storytelling, and a kind of mutual attempt to keep spirits up.

Ethel and Teddy and Steve Smith were up front,

and we all stayed in the back of the plane, nobody wanting to intrude on them, and we just reflected on ironies—like the fact that he was running for President, and now he was being brought back to New York on Air Force One, the Presidential jet. There was some anger when a reporter, who had come aboard as a friend, did a story about the mood of the plane. But that kind of anger fades pretty quickly; I don't guess any newsman could keep that kind of story to himself.

We landed at La Guardia, and there was, in a way, a moment of comic relief. The Kennedy family had made it very, very clear that it did not want politicians or family friends or anybody else grandstanding for attention. We had passed the word to Jim Tolan at La Guardia to keep Governor Rockefeller and Mayor Lindsay away from the family, since they'd both been rivals of a kind. We simply had our advance man putting people where we wanted them, and in most cases that meant keeping them away from the family.

We got the body into the hearse and the cars lined up, and Ethel actually told us to get going. And as we started into Manhattan for St. Patrick's Cathedral, I couldn't believe it. All along the highways, where crowds had never been, there were thousands and thousands of people, beneath the viaducts, along the Expressway where even Presidents never tried to pull crowds; they were all over, to line up and say a kind of farewell.

By the time we brought Robert Kennedy to St. Patrick's, the whole operation was in full gear, and it was almost like this was the biggest, last, critical rally of the campaign, with the same kinds of problems you get when advancing a political stop. We had enormous numbers of VIPs, and we had to figure out how to get them from St. Pat's to Penn Station for the train ride to Washington without holding up the family—the last thing we wanted was to have the family in that train waiting for everybody else to show up. So we had both telegrams and invitations that we sent to VIPs and other guests; we had checkpoints leading into the church, from the church to buses, from the buses at several points through Penn Station up to the funeral train itself. And everyone who was going to Washington got on those buses parked right outside St. Patrick's for the ride to Penn Station.

We spent hours negotiating with the Archdiocese about Communion—about whether we could restrict it for this service to the family, so that we wouldn't have to wait all that time—and they finally relented. We also had Secret Service agents descend on us, almost like Kennedy was one of the candidates who needed protection. The real reason for them, of course, was that Johnson was coming to the Mass and they wanted to plan a lot of the arrangements. Now you can call it jealousy or bottled-up anger and grief or ego, but I just said, "This Mass belongs to the Kennedys—Johnson's a guest."

But that had its limits. There were a number of people who had made a career out of hating Robert Kennedy whom we specifically did not want at that Mass—like Congressman Joe Resnik and Mayor Yorty. But when they showed up, there was nothing we could do—to force them physically to stay out would be to make a scene out of it. And nobody wanted to do that.

There was one weird incident. A guy came up to the door of St. Pat's and claimed he was a friend of mine, that he had a pass from me. The Secret Service checked him out and found a gun in his briefcase. An agent came up to me and asked, "Do you know this guy?" I said I did.

"He's a nut," I said also.

This fellow wanted to be Bob's upstate representative and was always a little bitter. He would hang around the office a lot; it's a type you see a lot of in politics, but we were taking no chances.

It was during this whole frenzy, this massive checking of details, that one reporter said what a lot of us were thinking.

"Isn't it a shame," he said, "all this talent going to waste—when with this operation they could be running the country, and here they are, preparing for a wake."

It was just after the Mass, I remember, that Ethel Kennedy came up to me. There may be women in the world with more courage and strength, but if there are, I haven't met them. We were at Penn Station, checking out credentials of the people boarding the train, and Ethel came up to me and stopped me.

She said: "Jerry, would you tell those who are working hardest to come to the house after the burial— we're going to have some brunch. Don't forget, the ones who are really working the hardest."

What can you say? With the commotion, with the million things that had to be on her mind, Ethel Kennedy wanted to do something for the guys who were working on this. All the way back to New York, all the way down to Washington, she was cheering up people who wanted to pull her spirits up—they found themselves turning to her.

With all of Bob's advance men working, that train pulled out of Penn Station not more than fifteen minutes after we brought Kennedy on. I found the Penn Central representative and just said "Go."

"We don't have everybody on," he said.

"I said, 'go,'" I answered, and we went. To this day, I don't know if we left anybody behind, but I never heard about it.

The way the world heard it and saw it, Robert Kennedy's last trip to Washington was a slow, solemn ride from New York down the northeast corridor. But it wasn't that easy. Like every other political stop I ever did, there were always the bureaucrats to contend with, who thought they knew what to do because this was the way the book said it should be done. And like every other part of politics, it took some doing to explain that what was really going on was a lot different than what the rule book said. I don't know, maybe that's the basic fact about the Bay of Pigs and Vietnam —it looks great on paper, but when you find out what's happening, you know the paper's all wrong.

I remember the worst example of this—one that caused authentic tragedy beyond the fact that it was Robert Kennedy's funeral. There was a communications system: W. J. Shields, a Penn Central official, and I, with a conductor, were between the car with Robert Kennedy and the family car. We had radio contact with the engineer. He in turn had radio contact with the Baltimore office. So at all times we had control over the train. The contract for this train said that it was to go "at a reasonable rate of speed."

Now to the Penn Central people, "a reasonable rate of speed" meant eighty miles an hour. Why? Because that's how fast trains went along Penn Central tracks on their way to Washington. The only trouble was, that schedule didn't usually plan for the presence of tens of thousands of people along the right of way, trying to get close to the train, to give some kind of good-by to Bobby. I remember that Shields, who'd seen the Roosevelt funeral train and Truman's campaign train, looked out at the crowds waving handkerchiefs and holding up signs that said "Farewell, Bobby," and he said, "I can't believe it. It's bigger than Roosevelt's. I just can't believe it."

I asked the engineer to slow the train down, and he did. But a little while later, past Newark, the train picked up its normal rate of speed. It seemed O.K. to me, and then it happened.

We came speeding through the station at Elizabeth, New Jersey, and the crowds were packed along the station platform on both sides. All of a sudden, around a sharp bend, an express train came barreling through on its way to New York. Somehow, with the crowd pushing forward to see the funeral train, people fell right into the path of that other train. It was horrible— silence and then screams. At first I thought they were

screams of grief for Kennedy, and then I saw this
woman falling in the path of the train, and I saw a
man leaning over her. It was an awful sight; she was
torn up badly and I couldn't believe she was alive.

I turned to Shields.

"We hit people," I said.

"You're right," Shields said, looking back.

"This can't happen," I muttered. It was like being
in shock. "We must have killed those people. Find out
what happened." We found out a few minutes later
that we'd hit five people, and we thought then that we
must have killed them all, although, as it turned out,
two died and the others were injured.

We first tried to get word to the press not to tell
Ethel when she came through the train to say hello to
people. Steve Smith told me to do whatever I had to
to stop anything else like this from happening. I went
to the conductor and said, "I want all the trains going
in the opposite direction stopped."

"I can't do that," he said.

"O.K.," I said, "either you stop them, or I'm gonna
stop this train."

The conductor relayed the word to the Baltimore
offices, and the answer came back that they couldn't
do it. So I leaned over into the microphone. I was
angry and numb and a lot of other things, and I talked
to Baltimore in a tone that I guess showed it.

"Let me tell you something," I snapped. "I don't
have time to argue with you, but if another train comes
by this one going in the opposite direction, we're not
moving. There must be a couple of hundred reporters
here. If your line wants to live with that kind of publicity, that you're killing people when we're telling
you not to kill people, all right. But we're not about to
kill another soul. We've got a dead man on this train,
and he wouldn't want anybody killed because of him.
If one more train goes by, I'm stopping."

Then I turned to the engineer.

"You're gonna go at the speed I tell you to go." And

every five minutes he'd give me his speed. We had the train slowed down to twelve miles an hour. By the time we got to Philadelphia, we were four hours late. And by now the spirit of that last train ride was developing.

There was a lot of laughter and storytelling on the train, just like on the plane coming back from Los Angeles; but every time we passed a crowd, that's when there'd be silence, and a lot of people started getting tears in their eyes and crying softly. You'd look out at all those faces—especially kids and people who looked poor—and you could see in their signs and in their faces (yes, we did get close enough to see their faces) that they were saying good-by to somebody they considered a friend. But we passed through all kinds of territory—suburbs, slums, farmland—and the crowds were always there.

People were making signs of the cross and throwing flowers against the side of the train. They held up signs they'd made saying "God Bless the Kennedys," or "Good-by, Bobby, We'll Miss You." At one station we went through, they were singing the "Battle Hymn of the Republic." You could hear it very clearly, and things like that would really hit you inside that train.

In a lot of places—North Philadelphia and Baltimore —the train passed through black ghettos, and the crowds there were enormous and dead-quiet. Of all the things I saw on that train ride, the faces of those black children, the little signs they'd made—I think that came closest to breaking me up. And in Baltimore, a crowd of young black men, with afros and very militant-looking postures, stood and saluted Bobby with the clenched fist. It was an odd gesture, since Bobby never claimed to be a radical or revolutionary, but it was somehow a way of them saying that they could respect Bobby by saluting him with *their* symbol, something that meant respect to them.

I remember going over a bridge—probably into Delaware—and there were twenty, maybe thirty boats lined up, sailboats, motorboats, all lying dead-still in the water. I remember passing by an athletic field of a school, and it must have been graduation day, and all along the fence between the track and the field, the kids were lined up in their graduation robes, and they took off their mortarboards when the train passed by. And the golf course we passed, where nobody was playing; everyone was just standing there, watching.

I guess the most ironic thing I saw was a small station we passed—I think in Pennsylvania—where American Legion and VFW members were lined up in their old uniforms, with big potbellies, and they were standing at attention and saluting. I couldn't help thinking of all the times in the campaign when Bobby said that Vietnam was a mistake, that we had to stop the war, and how it was the Legion and VFW that sent in letters and called him a traitor to his country. And here they were, standing at attention for this guy whom most of them would never have voted for.

The other thing that hit me was the spirit inside the train. As I mentioned, there was a lot of storytelling and laughter, and some tears, but the main thing was the unreality of it all—not just that Bob Kennedy was dead, but the realization of who was on the train. There were Ralph Abernathy from the Poor Peoples' March and ghetto spokesmen, and then there were Tom Watson from IBM and Benno Schmidt from Whitney Enterprises, two of the wealthiest men in the country, whom Bobby had gotten to help Bedford-Stuyvesant's self-help project.

There were Green Berets and Robert MacNamara, and peace demonstrators who thought MacNamara was a war criminal. A good part of this incredible collection of people had come together in one way or another behind his candidacy, others were there who liked him even if they weren't supporting him for President. We knew this was the last time we'd be together, that the opportunity would never occur again. People were saying, "You know, I hope this train ride never ends."

And that spirit grew even though the food ran out, the drinks ran out, the air conditioning broke down, and we got into Washington hours late. But somehow, I think everybody in that train wanted to hold onto that moment forever.

There was one more bad moment on that ride to Washington when we pulled into a station and a man climbed on top of a freight car on a side track to get a better view. He reached up to steady himself, grabbed electrified wires, and gave himself a terrible shock. For a minute we thought he'd killed himself, and I remember thinking, "My God, this train is jinxed." Not long after that, we got a call from Penn Central in Baltimore that we were running four hours late and that we had to pick up a normal rate of speed. That was when I learned that by a normal rate they meant eighty miles an hour, and I couldn't believe it.

The engineer himself was shocked at the order from Baltimore.

"My God," he said. "If I pick this speed up I'll kill thousands. People are getting in front of the train to put coins down, and then they're picking them up as a souvenir. They'll never get off the track in time. They're like cattle, they're moving so slowly. I'll kill thousands."

We simply countermanded that order, and we won the fight because the engineer finally got it through to Baltimore that the executives should stop looking at their papers and believe what was going on.

"I don't think you people believe me when I tell you the number of people who are on this thing," W. J. Shields said over the radio to Baltimore. "Your engineer says he'll kill thousands of people if he picks up speed. I can't impress on you the size of this. It's bigger than Roosevelt, it's the biggest thing I've ever seen and I'm not exaggerating. I wish you'd believe me."

So the guy in Baltimore said he'd have to check with higher authority; I swear, it was like talking with machines. They had no concept of what was going on. Finally, between our pleas and the engineer and the pictures that CBS was showing, they understood.

By the time we approached Washington, we were more than five hours late. A thought from the campaign kept running through my mind: how mad Bob Kennedy would get when we were running late. I remembered back to early May, a couple of days before the Indiana primary, when we were supposed to be in Whiting, Indiana, at 5 P.M. There were about ten thousand people there when we were supposed to arrive. The crowds along the way were so huge that we got word to Whiting we'd be four hours late. So the people went home, had dinner, came back, and by then there were twenty, maybe twenty-five thousand people waiting. I remembered how furious it would make Kennedy, how he said, "I don't think people should be kept waiting for me for four hours." And I thought, Well, Senator, we broke the record this time, and I thought of how angry he would have gotten.

Then we were approaching Union Station in Washington; it was pitch dark, but you could see the crowds in shadow, and the cars. And I remembered that as the campaign had gone on, this was what he had come to love: the neighborhood motorcades, the people in their own neighborhoods waiting for him, and how he'd come into their streets and sit on top of his car and wave to them, give them a little talk, try to answer questions even in the middle of a rally. Suddenly it hit me how much like a motorcade this train ride had been: into the slums, past the country-club golf courses, the suburbs, past factories and switching yards. It was like seeing all of it again. It was like it always had been, with the big crowds, everything but Kennedy saying, "Jerry, do we *have* to be this late?" or, "Let's get this thing going."

And then we were at Union Station, with President

Johnson, the Secret Service, the floodlights; it had the air of unreality again. We got the body out, the motorcade lined up, with a special bus for the press that had covered the entire campaign. We swung past the Justice Department, where he'd been Attorney General, passed the Senate Office Building, where his office had been, and stopped by the grounds of the Poor Peoples' Campaign encampment. There were thousands of people, lots of them with candles, all the way to Arlington Cemetery.

Even at the end there was a little humor and some class. It was pitch dark and the pallbearers couldn't find the place to set the casket down. Steve Smith, who was sort of leading them, didn't know where to go, and so they kind of walked around—almost as a matter of ritual, a last salute to Bob Kennedy—and then they just stopped and set the casket down near the grave.

Later I asked Steve Smith, "What the hell were you walking around for?" and he said, "You know, I had the feeling Bobby was looking at me through that coffin and saying, 'For Christ's sake, set me down. Don't you know where the hell you're going?'"

But to the thousands of people there, it looked like a farewell salute. Maybe that was the thing with the Kennedys—even with the confusion, they did it with class.

Later, at Hickory Hill, Steve came over and thanked me. I think that may have been the only time he ever did that. It was how the Kennedys worked; they thanked you more by putting their trust in you, by letting you do the job your own way as long as you proved to them you knew what you were doing.

I kept thinking all that night and for a very long time afterward that this was probably my last advance, and that if we'd planned it for two months it wouldn't have been as simple and as impressive. Although Bobby might have said something about the timing, I think he would have approved otherwise.

Humphrey in 1968: A Case History of the Importance of Advance Work

A lot of people who take an intellectual approach to politics like to moralize about political campaigns. "You're selling candidates like toothpaste," they say about media advertising. "All this hoopla has nothing to do with issues," they say about bands and rallies.

I think they're dead wrong. In the first place, that kind of political carrying-on has always taken place in Presidential elections. Read about the stump speeches for Andrew Jackson, or the torchlight parades in the nineteenth century, or the speeches and debates and country fairs, and it all comes down to the same thing: Much of politics is theater in America. Maybe it would be better if people sat back in their homes and read position papers on interest rates, but I don't think so. Anyway, with all the ghosts around, you wouldn't really get a feel for the guy. (And we've had ghost writers since George Washington's farewell address, which was written mostly by Alexander Hamilton.)

No, I think you *do* have to see a guy in the midst of a tangible, physical fight for the Presidency. Sure, it could be shorter, and we've got to figure out how to make TV equally available to everybody, but as far as personal campaigning goes, it's part of our politics. You had to see Tom Dewey to know he was a stiff; you had to see Nixon mouth those platitudes to know he was a phony. And candidates for the Presidency have to remember what people look like: they get isolated enough when they get to be President.

Then you move to the hard facts of political life, the facts the intellectual set likes to ignore or criticize. Most people do not think of politics in terms of issues. They vote for people who strike them as more honest, more trustworthy, more exciting, maybe sexier (call it more dynamic if you want to be polite about it).

That's why the advance work is so important. Because when you show people a man who can draw crowds, who can give them a sense of enthusiasm or excitement, you're giving them something recognizable, something understandable, while the debates about price supports or the Multi-Lateral Fleet are simply impossible to understand. And who knows?—maybe there *is* some link between a candidate's ability to draw crowds and persuade them, and his ability to lead a country.

What I *am* sure of is that advance work has an enormous impact on campaigns and their outcome. Because the press and the media judge candidates by the visceral, physical facts—how big was the crowd, how many people turned out, were they turned on or bored. Those stories create a sense of momentum or of failure. Those stories may persuade money-givers to go with a winner or hold back from a loser. When pollsters ask people who they're for, they remember what they've seen or read about a candidate and how he did. And those polls, in turn, can boost or flatten a candidate's morale, leading him to better speeches, or to dissatisfactions within a man's staff, gloomy leaks to the press, and the cycle of defeatism which can in fact create defeat. Think back to 1960, when John Kennedy started to get the crowds and the "jumpers," and the Republicans had to fight rumors that Nixon was thinking of himself as a loser. But if you want a perfect example of what advance work can do to a campaign, look at 1968. I'm willing to state flatly that the advance work on Hubert Humphrey's campaign made the difference; that with better advance work, he could have beaten Richard Nixon and been President today.

Now, that's a ludicrous statement at first glance. Had he lost by five or ten million votes, I wouldn't have said it. But as in 1960, when JFK won by only 100,000 votes and every water commissioner claimed he'd elected him, in a race as close as the Humphrey-Nixon race, any one factor can be singled out. Let me make my point that the advance work doomed Humphrey. Even if you don't accept that, you can at least see the consequences of good or bad advance work.

About two months after the death of Robert Kennedy, on August 14, 1968, to be exact, I met with Hubert Humphrey at the Waldorf-Astoria in New York City. I'd seen Humphrey in action before, usually on the other side of the fence, when I worked for John Kennedy in 1960 and for Bob Kennedy in 1968. Even before 1960, when I was with Senator Proxmire of Wisconsin, Hubert came into the state to help, and I'd had the chance to see him in action. His good and bad points never really changed—sincere, goodhearted, but always with a mouth that couldn't seem to close, and a quality of being the bumpkin. He reminded me somehow of the Great Gildersleeve, and the hardest problem he had in 1960 was to get people to think seriously of him as a President.

In 1964, after Johnson's landslide, a newsman close to the Kennedys suggested I might want to go with Humphrey, but it never really worked out. The bitterness from the Kennedy-Humphrey races in early 1960 was too great for some of Hubert's staff people, and the whole idea was dropped.

So this August of 1968 was my first direct meeting with Hubert in years—I don't think I'd seen him personally since the night of the West Virginia primary when I'd driven him back to his hotel after he'd lost to John Kennedy,

I walked in, and Hubert came into the room and

said, "Bruno, my old friend!" We talked for a while. He told me how he'd always wanted me to work for him, and that if he won, I could have any job in government. (I don't think he was talking about Attorney General or anything like that, but after some of Nixon's appointments you just can't tell.)

I also told the Vice-President that Robert Kennedy would have supported him over McCarthy if the nomination couldn't have gone to Kennedy. I wasn't just trying to make him feel good—it was what Bob Kennedy had told me, the night of April 4 in Indianapolis, shortly after King was shot. He'd been in a strange mood—probably thinking about Dallas—and he went to the rooms of a lot of staff people for a few minutes each, to talk or just to visit.

He'd said that night, "If I can't get it . . . if I don't have a crack at the nomination, I'm going to support Humphrey. I just really don't trust Gene McCarthy. I think he'd be a disaster for the country. Hubert's not that bad, he's qualified for the job. People deserve someone better than Gene McCarthy."

Humphrey remarked about how his relations with Kennedy had been good, and we talked more about his campaign. I told him I couldn't actively join his campaign because I had a Ford Foundation grant, but I did agree to advise his people on some ideas. But it was a bust. His advance men couldn't shake their suspicions that I was coming in to replace them, so no matter what I suggested, it was taken as an affront or as a kind of threat to their own jobs. You find that a lot in politics, and I guess you find it in business, too; but in this case I didn't want to be Humphrey's advance man, and if his staff had really believed that, it could have made an important difference. Because that first political swing of Hubert's after his nomination set his campaign back a month, and probably made the difference between his being President and professor of political science.

I went out with Humphrey on his first big political

swing after Labor Day—beginning on September ninth.
It's important to set the stage again, briefly. You remember the Democratic Convention. Apart from the
police riot, the bitterness of the McCarthy people, the
shambles that had been made of Hubert's normal liberal base of support, the fundamental fact was that the
convention had astounded people with its disorder.
Carl Albert squeaking like a mouse, Mayor Daley imi-
tating Rod Steiger as a gang boss, the disorder inside
and out—all had put a bad taste in the mouths of the
American people. The Republicans were saying, "How
can a party bring order to America if they can't even
bring order into their own convention?"

In addition, Hubert had been thought of as Lyndon's
puppet for four years; starting with Winston Chur-
chill's funeral (which an ill Johnson wouldn't let
Hubert go to), Humphrey was a pussy-whipped Vice-
President—and more than that, controlled by a man
whose popularity had vanished. So it was critical to
put the convention behind, to go out into a mass base
of support, to try to bind up intra-party wounds, and
to establish an independent base and an aggressive,
on-his-own Hubert Humphrey. It took forty-eight
hours to blow that whole idea out of the water.

We started out on September 9 for Philadelphia.
Nixon had received a tumultuous welcome in Chicago
on his first swing after the convention. He had gone
in at midday, with ready-made crowds, of course, but
the press reported that hundreds of thousands of
people turned out for Nixon. So the press traveling
with Humphrey was very keyed up about whether he
could pull crowds in his first real effort at going to
the people. I looked at the schedule and couldn't believe it. It read: "Ticker-tape parade in downtown
Philadelphia."

That's something you simply never put down on a
press schedule. It's like writing, "Spontaneous welcome
from thousands of grateful schoolchildren," in Mao
Tse-tung's diary. If a ticker-tape parade happens, it

happens. Even if you've planned it for a month, you always assume it's something that's spontaneous, not something that guys on top of buildings are directing. Anticipating a crowd is guaranteed to raise expectations in the press, and lower their opinion of the actual visit.

O.K., we land at Philadelphia's airport, on our *first stop*, and there's fifty people at the airport. Maybe, if Hubert's doing the counting. Fifty people? All during this flight the press has been talking "Nixon in Chicago" and this is what Humphrey gives them on his very first stop. I'd been pushing Hubert's people on this, asking them if they'd planned a big turnout.

"We've got this thing really locked up, Jerry," one guy told me. "We're going to have a wing-bang campaign in Philadelphia. It's going to be the biggest thing that ever happened." Well, fifty people is not quite the biggest thing that ever happened, even in Philadelphia.

We get out of the plane, Hubert waves to this vast throng, and we start to motorcade through the streets of Philadelphia, at about noon. Nobody's on the streets. Nobody! It's like the plague has struck. And six blocks from JFK Plaza, where the rally is taking place, they put Hubert in an open car, and that's like announcing to the press. "Hey, we expect a lot of people." If you *don't* expect people, don't even list a parade. Then if people do turn out, it's a surprise. But here they've got the parade listed, and nobody's out. The press is writing like mad, and they're not taking down license plates.

Oh, yeah—ticker tape! As we parade in the last six blocks, you can look up and see guys on rooftops throwing big bundles of confetti. This is the ticker-tape parade—really spontaneous and genuine-looking.

All along this route there are bunches of two, three, six, ten people. And when we get to JFK Plaza, there are three thousand people in a plaza that ten thousand couldn't fill. It's like picking a football stadium to hold a rally in.

Now this Philadelphia trip is object-lesson number one for an advance man. Why was it a bust? Because *Hubert's campaign hadn't changed direction since the convention. They were still looking for delegates.*

They got to Mayor James Tate, a big Democratic power in Pennsylvania and an early supporter of Humphrey. He says of course he'll help turn out the crowds, and he does what he could be expected to do. He has notices posted on City bulletin boards, urging people to go to the rally. But that's meaningless. Who's coordinating with the police, to make the Plaza accessible? Who's making sure people are coming out? Is there a phone operation? Is there a direct mailing? Tate—or any other local politician—has one interest, and that's to make sure people know he's running things. That's his payoff. But you can't really ask a mayor to tie up traffic and get his police force organized. You have to run things so that the candidate is getting the benefit of decisions.

Here's another example. The Philadelphia labor leaders were big for Humphrey before the convention. So you have to give them their jobs. But somebody from the candidate's staff has to oversee it. If you talk to them, they'll say, "Sure, we'll turn people out." But you never leave it up to them. You always have six independent operations going along with them. That way, if labor can pull, great—you'll have a really huge outpouring. If they can't, you're backstopped. But relying on power interests to get people interested in a campaign is madness. It won't work. You have to reach people directly, and that wasn't being done for Humphrey. He was preserving good relations with labor, not going over their heads to reach their people, all right—but people hadn't been aroused and they weren't there.

We left Philadelphia to fly west to Denver, Colorado, and on the plane the staff was celebrating as though Philadelphia was a huge victory. Maybe they thought

nobody would come out. They thought it was fantastic.
And I talked with them.

"You thought that was good?"

"Yeah, that was fine."

Meanwhile you can see the press stories. Disaster.
Nothing. Bust. Humphrey, who is a very hard man to
discourage, just sat there, but you could tell by looking
at him that he knew things weren't going right.

We land in Denver. Sixty people, with luck. Bob
Kennedy used to draw twenty times that many when
we landed in Denver to *refuel* at midnight. I know
Hubert didn't have the charisma or the cash, but, as
I think I can show later, you can still pull people.
Again, the Humphey people had left it to the organiza-
tions to pull for their man, and it wasn't working.

We motor into the hotel in Denver, and they've
set up barricades for two blocks. Insane! If you *know*
you will have mobs for a mile, *maybe* you set up barricades for six blocks. If you don't think you can pull
crowds for more than a block, don't have any barricades at all. Naturally, there are sawhorses for two
blocks and a little crowd about half a block from the
hotel entrance. It's a living advertisement to the press;
"SEE HOW MANY PEOPLE WE CAN'T TURN OUT
FOR HUBERT." Previously, of course, the labor leaders running this stop sent out written releases telling
reporters that they were going to have thousands of
people along the way. Sure, it's a gimmick to tell the
press a thousand people will show up when you think
that five thousand will. But what kind of trick is it to
promise fifty thousand when you can't pull one thousand?

We drive up to the hotel. Humphrey gets out. A
few people clap. You know the Zen Buddhist question, What is the sound of one hand clapping? I've
got a better one. What is the sound of three people
clapping for the Democratic presidential nominee on
his first campaign trip? Answer: Horrible. We go into
the hotel, and Humphrey goes to a ballroom there to

speak to union delegates. It's half full, because only delegates can attend. Now, there are two choices here. Either you find a smaller hall, or you let other people inside to listen to Hubert. It's not a secret meeting, but it's only half filled. And then, *two hours later*, he goes into the same hall for a rally, the same faces are there —and it's half full again.

They thought—the Democrats, the Mine Workers, whoever ran that show—they would pull people with an ad in the paper. Not so. So for the second time in two hours, Humphrey walks into a half-filled hall. Now get this. He's supposed to arrive at 7 P.M. At *five minutes* to seven, with the press there, a guy climbs on stage and hands out homemade signs. They're still passing out those signs when Hubert walks in. My God, I'm dying! Then, as Humphrey walks to the stage, some guy booms into the mike, "All right, now start yelling!" And bam! in this half-filled room, all of a sudden they're cheering and waving signs. Who are they impressing? The press? They're going up the wall. Hubert? He's a little starry-eyed, but he's not blind. And the press is saying the damn campaign's over.

So that's it for the night. Now Hubert doesn't help this. Bob Kennedy would be deflated by a small crowd, and, in a way, that was a help. He'd be quieter, and you knew he understood the size and mood of the crowd, even if he might be angry about it later. But with Humphrey it made no difference. He'd get up before four people and a fire hydrant and talk for an hour like he was in Yankee Stadium. And that only intensified his image as a mouth.

So we bid farewell to Denver and landed in Los Angeles, at the West Imperial Terminal, the place for charter flights, where no one draws crowds. The only time I saw a real crowd there was three months earlier, when they took Robert Kennedy's body back to New York. But the Humphrey people had billed a "GREET HUBERT HUMPHREY" rally at this airport in Outer Mongolia. His first stop in the biggest state in the Union, his first rally as nominee in California, and less than a hundred people showed up. There were party people there, the people who backed Hubert and got 12 percent of the vote in the California primary, and it was pitiful. And the next thing we did was to spend the night in the Ambassador Hotel, where Robert Kennedy had been shot.

It was unbelievable. The press couldn't understand it, since it had to offend anybody who had been close to Kennedy or worked for him. It wasn't deliberate or malicious, simply a stupid oversight, and it hurt politically, because it was on the minds of the press, especially those who had covered Robert Kennedy. I damn near didn't go there, but we were leaving early, and I figured it would create another problem on top of those we already had.

The next morning we start campaigning in California. We spend an hour driving on the freeways to our first stop, a taping for a local TV station. Everywhere Bob Kennedy had gone, those shows had come to him—setting up in a room in the hotel. You can call it arrogance if you want to, but a man running for President has just so much time—and a nominee even less. So there goes an hour, for a local taping. Then we go out to TRW electronics plant—another hour on the freeways—to speak at their regular speakers' forum. The crowd was four thousand—about half of what Bob Kennedy pulled. Please don't misunderstand; *I'm* comparing turnouts because *the press* was comparing them, and every mention of the relative pull was another nail in Hubert's balloon. Believe it or not, that was his first major speech.

Now we go back to the airport and take off for Houston, Texas. On that whole swing to the West, we've seen less than ten thousand people—roughly two persons per mile traveled.

We land in Houston. Biggest airport crowd of the trip so far, about a thousand. Everyone thinks this is fantastic, greatest crowd since the Sermon on the

Mount. Now watch what happens. We hit the hotel at 7 P.M. At 8 P.M. we go to a reception for a judge in the Crystal Ballroom, where Humphrey is introduced by a former Democratic congressman. At 8:30 P.M. Humphrey goes to the third floor for a reception with about twenty civic leaders. Then at 9 P.M. Humphrey goes back to his suite for a color photo session with the "top photographers" of the Houston newspapers. Man, I don't care if it's Margaret Bourke-White, that's one hell of a waste of time. Now it's 9:30 P.M. and Vice-President and Mrs. Humphrey go to the Crystal Ballroom for a kickoff reception for 750 supporters. At 10:30 P.M. the Humphreys go up to the eighteenth floor to meet with Negro leaders. That's his visit to Texas, his first visit. Five appearances in one hotel, no rallies, no efforts to get out and stir up enthusiasm for himself in a key state.

Now I know what can be said. I worked for John and Robert Kennedy, two men who at one time or another stirred up more excitement than any other politician of their time. But that doesn't matter. Of course you can't match the Kennedy crowd appeal, so don't try. But *do* try for the things that can build a crowd. Go into the field houses of high schools (less likelihood of disruptions than at colleges, for Hubert) and pull the kids. I know they can't vote, but they can bring their parents, and if you have a large crowd cheering 'for you, that's more important in the first few days than almost anything else. And if you can't draw at all, don't.

If you're going to meet with leaders, as in Houston, what's the point of five separate meetings? You pull them together. You *demonstrate* that you can bring people together by bringing them together. And no matter what people say, they'll damn well come together if it's the next President of the United States they're meeting.

Now comes the one point on substance that I think I'm qualified to make. Between Houston and his plane flight to New Orleans, Humphrey made a statement about Vietnam. He advocated troop withdrawal. The next morning President Johnson went to the American Legion Convention and undercut Humphrey totally by saying something like, "Anybody who's promising troop withdrawals doesn't know what he's talking about." Hubert couldn't understand it. He almost had tears in his eyes.

"What did you think about what Johnson did to me? . . . He really cut me up," Hubert said. "You know," he went on, "before I made that statement I called Clark Clifford [then Secretary of Defense] and he told me to go ahead and say that. I checked it out with the White House, and they all told me to go ahead and make it. Why is it so bad that I'm giving a little bit to the Kennedy people to let them know that I really want to think like they do on Vietnam?

He was really upset, asking, "Why did he have to do this to me? I really didn't deserve it." And he asked me what I thought he should do.

Like I say, I'm no expert on Vietnam. In fact, mostly I got asked about substantial issues, only as a matter of ego massage—you know, John or Robert Kennedy were trying to let me know they trusted me, rather than really wanting to know what I thought. But in this case, I told Humphrey, and I still think it could have made a difference early. I told him to really blast Lyndon, to say, "When I'm President, I'm going to bring peace to Vietnam the way I think it has to be done."

That would have accomplished two things right off the bat. First, a feud between Humphrey and Johnson would have been tremendously encouraging to the anti-war forces, the Kennedy and McCarthy people, who were looking for some solace after the assassination and that horrible convention. Second, and maybe more important, *it would have established Humphrey as his own man.* Hawk or dove or whatever, people worried about Humphrey being under Lyndon's control. Lyndon wasn't a popular President anymore. People would have leaped at some early signs that Hubert Humphrey was a tougher cookie than we had given him credit for.

If you remember, it was when Humphrey gave his "I would stop the bombing" speech in Salt Lake City that things began to change. Kids got friendlier—the anti-war people started giving their endorsements—and the campaign got moving. I think if that break—more open and tougher—had come in the first swing, it would have made up for much of the bad publicity about the crowds. But it didn't.

In case you think it's all speculation that crowds would have come out for Humphrey, the answer is that they did, in the later weeks of the campaign, after Salt Lake City and after excitement built up. And, to be blunt and immodest about the whole thing, we did it for Humphrey in Utica, New York. That was the first overflow crowd he had, with more than four thousand people in the War Memorial and two thousand outside. The press couldn't believe it, and neither could Humphrey. This was a kind of double-interest thing on my part. I was working for the mayor of Utica, Dominick Assaio, who was running for reelection, and I convinced Larry O'Brien to bring Humphrey through Utica instead of Syracuse. That's like asking the Pope to endorse Enovid, it's so heretical—every candidate always goes through Syracuse and Buffalo upstate. But I thought it would be good for my man, and also what we could pull for Humphrey. And we did—with very basic techniques, with telephone calls and invitations, by getting people involved. (I also persuaded Humphrey's people that it would be great to bring a grant from the Department of Housing and Urban Development for Utica, which Humphrey did.)

I do admit it's easier for an advance man to pull a crowd for the Kennedys than for a Humphrey, but it isn't that much different. And it's not as though the Kennedys had any divine magic on their side. John

Kennedy used to walk down the streets of Wisconsin villiages *looking* for people to shake hands with. The magic started after some very hard work and very lonely days of campaigning. It can be done—if the people working for a candidate don't put their faith in the promises of labor, or politicians, or any other special group more interested in protecting their hides than in pulling people for a Presidential candidate.

The most important lesson to be learned from this first fiasco of Humphrey's was what it did to the campaign. And when you understand this, you can see why candidates and their staffs worry more about crowds than about issues.

If you could make a deal with the press and TV, if you had them agree, "We won't mention crowd sizes, we won't show any pictures of crowds. We'll just run items about the candidates talking about issues," I'd pack up and go home tomorrow. I think it would be bad for politics and bad for the country, because I think politicians are far more revealing among people than in a TV studio—but I admit that you could in theory wipe out crowds as an important item in campaigns.

However, it doesn't work that way.

Reporters write about who pulls the biggest crowds. TV cameras show the candidates speaking before full or empty halls. They catch excitement or boredom, followers or indifferent loungers who just want the candidate to shut up. And that feeds into a whole complicated series of reactions.

Take the polls, for instance. They ask a guy who he thinks is best qualified to be President. To an average voter, that's a damn hard question. Maybe he cares about issues or even a certain issue. But among people who aren't hardcore Republicans or Democrats, liber-als or conservatives, the decision is a vague one. It's highly likely to be shaped by images, by things barely remembered. And it's more than likely to be shaped by what the guy remembers reading or seeing. He may say to himself: "Do I want to be for the guy who had all those people cheering for him in Chicago, or the guy who looked like he was in the middle of a funeral in Philadelphia?" And it's pretty clear what his answer will be. He'll say, "I think Nixon could do the better job."

The early polls did show Nixon with an enormous lead. Now other things happen, and don't happen. Like money. Nobody except a guy's mother would give money to a certain, absolute loser. There just wasn't any money for Humphrey, because nobody thought he could win. And that in turn meant no money for TV until the last week, no money for brochures and buttons, no money for good advance (yes, it sometimes *does* take money), and a campaign that never got unstuck until the last few weeks. If the advance had been better earlier, the polls would have been better earlier, the money would have come in sooner, and the campaign just might have been won.

Now take another factor. A lot of Democrats who ran in 1968 ran as anti-war candidates: O'Dwyer in New York for the Senate, McGovern for reelection from South Dakota. Some of them—particularly Congressional candidates in New York and California, where peace sentiment was strong—were under pressure to endorse or not endorse Humphrey. For the whole first month of the campaign, there was no pull for them to go with Humphrey—he was a sure loser. It's entirely possible that with a more vigorous campaign, with an open break with Johnson on the war, you'd have gotten far more excitement among Democrats—by giving them a reason to get behind Humphrey. As it turned out, O'Dwyer and McCarthy both sort of endorsed Hubert a few days before the election. But a firmer, earlier endorsement—which a break with Lyndon could have helped—would have gone a long way toward healing those intra-party wounds and maybe getting Humphrey some of the backing he needed in those early days.

That's one of the biggest things about crowds that political scientists and intellectuals miss. It's not just pre-planned excitement, although God knows you do have to plant to get out "spontaneous" crowds, even for charismatic leaders. But campaigns tell you if a candidate and his staff know what they're doing. (Kennedy used to say in the Senate, "How can I get out of Vietnam if I can't get the mail out of my own office?" You might ask, "How can a man run the country if he can't run a campaign?")

Also, I think campaigns—the way a candidate handles himself running for office—tells you a lot about what kind of a President he'll be. I think Bob Kennedy would have been a President in constant motion, going into migrant camps and back to Mississippi, into cities to see community action in motion, breaking through bureaucracy. And I think Nixon's campaign was a perfect example of what kind of President he'd be. People talked about his isolation after Cambodia. Hell, what was it when they packed the first ten rows of halls with Nixon girls, and put up mikes to make the cheers sound louder, and kept everybody with a beard out of his Madison Square Garden rally, and ran the damn campaign like it was a show for a new kitchen range? You knew Nixon had no feel for the country by the way he campaigned for the job of leading it.

Humphrey had another kind of drawback. It was a campaign of inefficiency and incompetence for the first month or so. And much as you know that voters don't know the issues or positions in detail, they *can* sense things about a man—the sense that Humphrey was weak and indecisive and somehow not strong enough to run things. That may well have been an unfair picture—but that's how it *looked* to America and that was enough to sink him for the first half of the campaign. Better advance work could have made a better campaign, a better candidate, and maybe a different *President*.

How Lindsay Will Beat Nixon in 1972

One of the first things you learn in politics is that the guys who like to think of themselves as the hard-nosed, tough-minded realists are almost always wrong—because they're always right about the *last* campaign. John Kennedy couldn't win in West Virginia in 1960; a Catholic couldn't be elected President; you couldn't challenge a President within your own party.

The line today is that Richard Nixon is a great politician, skilled, shrewd, cunning. Bull. Richard Nixon is one of the really bad political minds around today.

Here's a guy that was Vice-President for eight years under one of the most popular people ever to be President, in a time when there was no war and no real chaos in the country, running against a young, inexperienced Catholic, and losing. Here's a guy who goes back to his home state two years later and gets killed for governor. And here's a guy whose greatest opposition is assassinated, who's running against the weakest Presidential candidate the Democrats have put up since Alton B. Parker, at a time when the entire nation is fed up with a war and internal rioting, a guy with an absolutely unlimited campaign budget against a bankrupt opponent, who comes into Labor Day with a totally intolerable, chaotic Democratic Convention which has split the Democrats eight ways from Tuesday—and he goes from a ten-million to a half-million vote lead in eight weeks.

If that's political skill, I'm Cary Grant.

At the bottom line, people really don't like Richard Nixon. That's really what a lot of politics is all about: a basic, instinctive sense that you like a guy or you don't. If Lyndon Johnson had built that sense of trust with the people, if he hadn't been looked on as a kind of fixer, it would have been a lot harder to send him back to Texas. Nixon has that same core liability; people don't really care about him. If you want a clue to his persistent habit of surrounding himself with symbols of affection—from Bob Hope to Billy Graham (the official delegate from God to the Republican Convention)—it's because he knows he's not really liked. Maybe he thinks it can happen by osmosis.

You could see the Nixon understanding of his own limits in the 1968 campaign. He learned in 1960 that he couldn't draw a crowd, that he couldn't fight somebody with real popular appeal in the streets. People read that Kennedy's crowds were bigger and more enthusiastic than Nixon's—so *they* wanted to be part of the action. Then Nixon's crowds started dropping off, and the press picked that up; his speeches became a little boring, and the staff started arguing among themselves—and there went the campaign.

Anyway, Nixon's people knew this in 1968. They knew they couldn't stage a ten-mile motorcade for him, but they could draw crowds for three blocks. And here's where the psychology of crowds comes in. They would put up sawhorses, signs, bands, all of it, but *only* for a three-block period. And so newsmen wouldn't ask, "How come there's no crowds for ten miles?" They'd say, "Wow, that's a crowd that's packed ten deep!' Sure it is . . . for three blocks. But on TV, and for the news stories, that was enough. They'd begin the motorcade three blocks before it ended; and they had the money to bus in people, to get bands moved in and confetti thrown, and to create a feeling that Nixon was being mobbed and cheered spontaneously.

They also knew how to use captured crowds. That, plus bussed-in Nixon Girls and all the rest, is all you need. They knew enough not to *try* for crowds at bad times. With Robert Kennedy, if we landed in Cactus Bush at 3 A.M., we'd try for a rally and people would come, even without the techniques. But Nixon's rallies —for time, for location—it was one rally, one motorcade, all timed and planned to look like a happy, cheering throng emotionally pouring out their hearts for Dick Nixon.

Now all of this is very clever. But it creates one hell of a problem. I've argued again and again, and I'll do it again here, that with all the importance of TV and the media, you can't skip real, honest-to-God personal confrontations, personal contact with people. Whether it's John Kennedy in West Virginia or Robert Kennedy seeing the faces in Indiana and Nebraska, there's something real that cuts through all the gimmicks and the planning when a candidate is really meeting face-to-face with people.

When you do it Nixon's way, you're going to get a candidate who has no goddamn feeling—no feeling for the issues, no feeling for people. You're going to get a Reagan—a propped-up, smiling doll, or a frowning, serious, I-mean-business doll, with nothing to back it up. You're going to phony it up. And that's the danger, for the country and also politically.

Because you can't really phony up the people. Sure, you can play with them or use carefully planned "spontaneous" signs, or one of the hundreds of political tricks. But they want to hear somebody who understands what's on their minds. If you're talking to somebody who's hungry, whose kids don't have enough to eat, if you're talking to somebody who may be drafted over to Vietnam, or whose kid's at a college where they're demonstrating, you can't bull him. You can see concern in people's faces and in their questions, if you let them ask questions. And that makes for a better man, a better President. Taking Nixon today, you can prop him up any way you want. And people aren't going to buy it much longer.

The question is, how do you beat him and whom do you beat him with? My answer is, you beat him by forcing the press, and then the people, to see through Nixon's charade by giving them a candidate who can *really* go to the people, more than that who has charisma, and something more than that—who can run tougher and be tougher and go into more places than Nixon. I think right now the guy is John Lindsay. And I think he will run and win as a Democrat in 1972.

Right away I can hear all the pros telling me that this is insane, that John Lindsay couldn't win, that he couldn't even come close to the nomination, that he isn't even a Democrat now, that organized labor's all against him, that he's poison in the South, that the silent majority-type hates his guts. All of which (or most of which) is true at present and all of which doesn't make one damn bit of difference.

I think Lindsay proved what he could do in the 1969 mayoral campaign. They took a poll at the start of that year—it was after the school strike and the whole black-Jewish dispute and the snowstorm when he was out of town—right after the worst of it—and it reported 75 percent of New York's voters would take anybody instead of Lindsay. Then in June he lost the Republican primary and all he had was the Liberal party, which is just a shell. Now if John Lindsay had pulled a Nixon campaign, if he had just put on those TV commercials (and they were great commercials, by the way) and isolated himself, I don't think he'd have won. Because even *after* people see those commercials, they want to see Lindsay, they want to ask him, "Do you really think you've learned from your mistakes?" "How come my garbage is never picked up until midnight?" "What are you going to do about the blacks taking over the schools?"

And Lindsay did exactly the right thing. He went into Queens, to the same street where they booed him for the snow snafu, and he said, "Yes, I really loused it up, but it isn't going to happen again, and these fifty new snowplows we just bought are *why* it isn't going to happen again." He had to go into those synagogues in Flatbush, in the same neighborhood they drove him out of in 1968, and talk to angry people, and talk about anti-Semitism to people who were literally concerned that SNCC and the Ford Foundation were planning another pogrom, another Dachau. I think Lindsay won because people could listen to him, could reach the inaccessible leader, because the White Knight got up off his horse, and because they saw the humanity in the guy. And no matter how big the office is, President or what have you, that quality is what people really respond to.

That, I think, is the clue to how John Lindsay will win in 1972. He's got the ability to beat Nixon on the real issues that turn elections: trust, confidence, and humanity.

In a funny kind of way, elections give candidates the chance to break up myths which separate them from people or to make up myths that ruin them. George Romney in 1968 let one word slip—"brainwash"—and he was a fool, and an incompetent in the eyes of the country; the press began putting every word of his under a microscope, and once that happens, any candidate—any man who speaks in public—is finished.

Look at John Kennedy in 1960. He was a Catholic. And hard as it is to remember, there were a lot of places in America where a Catholic was considered a subversive, who would smuggle the Pope into Washington the day after he was inaugurated. So he went into West Virginia, and just the idea of going to people, talking with them informally, helped dispel that myth; because when you talk with a guy, laugh at his jokes, listen to his ideas, even if you don't agree with everything he says, he stops being a villain. You forget to hate him. And that's what John Kennedy did in West Virginia, and at a meeting of Houston ministers, which was run as a half-hour TV commercial in Bible Belt states because it showed Kennedy as he *was*, talking right out at the issue which was in the back of everybody's minds.

Or think about Bob Kennedy in 1968. What was his myth? Ruthless—a cold, cynical, calculating street fighter. You can't knock that out of people with commercials, because people *really* don't believe what they see on TV (which is why they instinctively believe Agnew's line about a biased press). It's something they turn on and that comes at them, from out there somewhere. So for Bob Kennedy, the street route was critical. And the whistle-stop—my God, that was a perfect thing for RFK to use, in half a dozen ways. First, it brought you into the real Middle America, the places left behind by jet planes and the death of railroads and new industrial plants. Many of these towns had never seen a Presidential candidate for fifty or sixty years, much less a Kennedy. Here was that guy who was a New Yorker, a jet-setter, an alien, with all those crazy ideas about blacks and blood for the Viet Cong, and here he was, in Wabash or whatever. And Kennedy would always say, "Has McCarthy been here? Did Hubert come here?" There'd be all these people— different from Bob Kennedy in every way, farmers with red faces and rough hands, guys who worked in factories—who'd be at the back of the train, and there was Bob Kennedy teasing them, joshing with them, talking about why he wanted to be President, and no matter what else they thought, the "ruthless" tag dropped right away. Kennedy was a warm, affectionate man who really loved his country, and that came across in those stops.

Now think about the myths in the way of John Lindsay, and you'll begin to see the outlines of his kind of campaign. (I'm assuming, by the way, that he goes as a Democrat. I don't think a fourth-party route is impossible, especially if there's direct election of a President by 1972, but it seems a long shot right now; anyway, a lot of this strategy can be carried over into an independent campaign.)

Myth No. 1: Lindsay is concerned only about New York City. He doesn't understand the real America.

There's a lot of anti-New York City sentiment in the rest of America, a feeling that New York is the wicked big city, where the very rich manipulate the rest of us. It's a kind of populist strain in American life, which goes back at least to LaFollette and Bryan, maybe all the way to Andrew Jackson. A lot of people outside of the big city think—and a lot of times they're right— that New York is where all the people screwing them live. That's where they sell us the machines that break down, that's where they hold the mortgage on my house, that's where those welfare chiselers are taking my tax money. And of course, you still have the left-over strains of anti-Semitism and anti-black feeling— you know, New York is where all those minorities live —and it's also the place where they sell all this pornography. Now that's just a little bit oversimplified, but it's the kind of myth that can build up, and even if somebody believes it a little bit, that can hurt.

If *for no other reason,* Lindsay has to go to the people to show them what kind of a guy he is. He's not this cold-hearted bastard from the Big City, he's a good-looking, friendly guy, like the rest of us. He's already moved on that front within New York State. For four years Lindsay went up to Albany and screamed for more money and posture—and all Governor Rockefeller had to do was say, "See? Here's the mayor of the big city trying to glom off our money," and that was that.

Now, in early 1970, Lindsay met with the mayors of the five other big cities in New York State. They decided to make a joint pitch: that the same money pressures on New York City were hitting Albany and Syracuse and Rochester and Buffalo and Yonkers. These five other mayors—all Democrats—stuck together with Lindsay, and they beat Rocky's brains in to get a new formula for state aid to cities. And Lindsay also got the support of the state conference of mayors, which meant even the small towns were with him.

That's the kind of issue you can take to the country. "Look, you don't have to tell *me* about too much power in Washington. I suffer from that every day. I want that money put back into towns and suburbs and villages and cities—for their schools and hospitals and roads. Because it's no different in New York than in Peoria. All of us are struggling for the same things."

So he's got that kind of record and that kind of approach, *if* he goes to the people with it, if he makes it clear that his city's in the same bind they are: for more cops and more services and less local property taxes.

Also, in a way, this anti-New York City thing is a two-way street. You take the average guy knocking New York City and ask him if he'd like to go to New York, he'll be on that plane in four seconds flat. They all want to be there, and even if they're just traveling through the city, they tell their friends. It's the center, for better or worse, and there's a fascination with it that's nationwide. So Lindsay's New York identification is a plus, not a minus, always provided Lindsay knows how to reach out and identify with the rest of the country.

Myth No. 2: Lindsay can't govern New York City, so he can't govern the United States.

Here, again, that anti-New York City feeling can have a boomerang effect. If Nixon tried to make the conditions in New York City an issue, a lot of people would simply brush it off. "What the hell," you hear people say, "New York City is completely ungovernable anyway. You can't blame Lindsay for not building a paradise." In other words, the same things that people use to put down the city also let them excuse a lot of the failures of any mayor. And Lindsay would be no exception.

Furthermore, Lindsay can say, "You're right, Dick Nixon, there *is* too much garbage and too much welfare and too much crime in New York. And you want to know one of the reasons why? It's because you're taking nine billion dollars a year from my city and putting that money into the war and defense and space. One flight to the moon is the entire police budget of New York for a year. It could build five hundred schools. One month of that war in Vietnam is the total budget for three years in Wyoming." That whole line, also, draws some response from other communities—any place where local taxes are too high. It's a funny kind of bridge between liberal and conservative pitches. Taxes are too high, the federal government *is* too powerful, and if we could stop the war and cut these defense and space budgets, we could make New York and the rest of the country a lot better.

Also, you could use much of the success of John Lindsay to identify him with the rest of the country—his idea of using police more sensibly; his concern for the environment, even in a place like New York City, and the riot thing, which is a whole separate, major plus. So, in one sense, the fact that Lindsay has been wrestling with the roughest city in the country is going to raise his stature; people will look at him and almost automatically credit him with guts, which, by the way, is something that few people can find in Nixon.

Myth No. 3: Lindsay is the black man's candidate. He'll totally turn off white middle-class America.

There's no question that Lindsay has a long way to go with the working-class people of New York City. Part of the hardhat explosion in May, 1970, was clearly an anti-Lindsay thing, with signs like "Lindsay Is a

Faggot" and "Impeach the Red Mayor." However, as far as the black issue goes, it is another one of those "facts" our political geniuses recite over and over until they're proven wrong.

Look at Bob Kennedy in 1968. When he came into the race, all the prestige writers started talking about how Robert Kennedy would divide the nation, how he was too identified with black people and dissent. So what happened? He went into Indiana—home of the American Legion, stronghold of the Klan for years, center of places like Gary and Hammond, where there was a huge vote for George Wallace in *1964*—and he got big wins in all those white working-class city districts. Why? Just because he was Catholic? Just because he was John Kennedy's brother? Not on your life.

In a strange sort of way, they voted for Bob Kennedy in part *because* he could talk to black people, *because* they trusted him. You could hear it again and again: the conviction that Kennedy could take care of the problem, and what they wanted was a President who was tough enough to solve the problem any way it had to be solved. George Wallace told them you could do it with a police-state mentality. Bob Kennedy said it would take jobs and help. What they wouldn't stand for, these white working-class people, was more liberal bull with welfare and poverty programs that were phony. But if Kennedy would get the country away from riots and burnings, fine, they'd trust him.

Now, at least as far as the black problem goes, Lindsay has that clearly on his side. I know people talk about him giving New York away, but that's nonsense—and more important, it's not a pervasive thought outside New York City. If Lindsay can demonstrate a campaign that goes everywhere—to the white, black, poor, workingman, suburb—then the black support in most places will become an asset.

Lindsay has a much more serious problem with the college kids—because the resentment is much greater.

You know, if you talk to policemen or steelworkers, they may make racist remarks, but they really know what life is like for blacks. They'll say, "God, if I had to live like that, if my kids had to go to schools like in those neighborhoods, I'd riot too." They can identify with hard times, with being poor and living in crummy housing, because a lot of whites aren't that far away from Depression conditions.

But when they see the kids—the children of rich or comfortable people, who have it made—when they see those kids burning down colleges that a steelworker could never go to, that's when they really hit the roof. The dislike of those kids and everything they represent to an ordinary American—the hair, the pot, the sex—that whole sense of anger and envy and bitterness all wrapped up is an explosive mixture. No politician —especially one like Lindsay, who is glamorous and confident—can afford to be looked at as the candidate of those kids. That's what Lindsay has to watch out for, far more than the issue of being "the black man's candidate."

Now those, I think, are some of the myths about a Lindsay-type Presidential candidacy. But there's one basic thing about how Americans vote for a President that works entirely in Lindsay's favor, *if* the campaign is run right. And it can be described in one word: excitement.

I *don't* mean that Presidential campaigns are circuses. That's exactly wrong. People will not vote for a man with the most hoopla, at least not if it's phony or staged. But, as I must say once again, they will go with the guy who seems to be exciting the people, who can draw crowds *and* talk to those crowds, deal with them as people and not things, answer their questions, argue with them, inspire them. Glamour, charisma, whatever you call it—it's a starting point and also a dangerous thing. Because it will get people interested in a guy, and *then* he has to prove that he's more than a pretty boy, that he can run hard and talk honestly and convince them.

Take, for instance, John Kennedy in 1960. He had a sort of glamour, judging by the newspaper and magazine stories. He was attractive, something like a star, and people were curious to see him. At the beginning, maybe that was all he had. But once the interest was there, there were other things that drew people to him, such as his seeing poverty in West Virginia and talking about it with shock and anger, the Houston ministers' appearance, and the debates with Nixon—all these things told people, "Yeah, he's pretty, but he cares, he's got guts, he's at least as mature and smart as Nixon."

Now that ability to excite interest is something that Lindsay already has. You can hear Democrats in a lot of places talking about him, saying, "Hey, what about Lindsay?" He's been put into the Gallup poll stakes as a possible Democratic candidate, and that act *alone* is critically helpful to Lindsay. He is, in other words, a possibility, in people's minds, as a candidate for President in 1972, and he has the excitement and the glamour to keep that interest alive.

And more important: he has more of it than Nixon will have, even as an incumbent President in 1972.* I saw some of Nixon's efforts in 1968, and the staged quality of his appearances are still very much in evidence. The contrast between Nixon and an open, spontaneous campaign that Lindsay could put together would be apparent, even to the national press, which is usually as gullible as a Billy Graham audience.

* All of this assumes that Nixon will run again and be nominated in 1972. It's possible that he will pull a Johnson or be defeated by a Reagan type if the country is in a full-scale depression by then. But given Nixon's lust for the trappings of power, his glee when they strike up "Hail to the Chief" and haul him from Florida, and the closed nature of the Republican party, we can assume that Nixon will run unless fate intervenes.

And once they started to point out the difference, you would have another 1960—a demoralized Nixon campaign, a sense of momentum around Lindsay, and possibly even a sense of panic which seems to grip Nixon during tough times. To put it together, Lindsay would need to work hard, he would need luck, and he would need to be a tough enough man and candidate not to make the kinds of mistakes that could finish him off before he even started to run. But I think he could do it. And this, in as much detail as it's possible to go into now, would be how it could be put together.

The worst thing that could happen to Lindsay would be for somebody to start planning a full-scale, fireworks-and-bunting Presidential campaign. People are smarter than politicians give them credit for. In fact, people are smarter than most politicians, period. They know when someone is trying to stuff himself down their throats. In this period Lindsay will have to move carefully and well. If he rushes into everything, if his people say yes to everything that looks good, he's going to be destroyed. And it all plugs into one question: *Can he attract the rest of the nation?* He can walk in shirt sleeves through Harlem, but can he get a response in Gary, Indiana?

He's already shown something of this in his trip to Berkeley in April, 1970. He didn't come on as Superhero for the kids, but he got a good reception there and at Stanford, and that reminded a lot of people that there aren't that many politicians who can get listened to and applauded on campuses. He also, you know, went to a dinner of the California Alumni Association —which is one kind of establishment group—and got a very good reception.

All through 1971 Lindsay should be speaking to different kinds of groups in different kinds of states: primary states and non-primary ones. He should definitely go before a labor group, maybe a national union meeting somewhere in the Midwest, one that he has some kind of simpatico with, like the United

Auto Workers or a Hospital Workers' Union. The construction trades would murder him right now, and I don't think the national police officers' union would be exactly right, either. But some union group would help, where he could talk, for example, about the similarity of economic pressures on the wage earner and on big cities. He does very well with senior citizens, so a speech to a group of them in California or Indiana would make sense. He's a natural for the League of Women Voters, which was his original constituency in New York City, or any other good government group.

The key element in all this is to build a following for Lindsay—not really enormous hoopla, but a quieter and broader kind—so people in 1971 will begin to say: "Oh, Lindsay, yeah. My brother saw him at a union meeting and liked him"; "Lindsay? He wants to improve Social Security." I wouldn't try for an emotional, all-out series of receptions. First, I don't know that Lindsay would be that good at that sort of thing; second, they might not be possible to arrange; and third, it's not the kind of experience a man who wants to be President needs right away. The isolation around candidates and Presidents is bad enough already. What anyone—Lindsay and the rest—needs now is a chance to meet people, to listen, to argue back and forth. And politically, it's enough that there's a following building up, that people want to hear what Lindsay has to say.

Also, throughout 1971 there should be more visible and dramatic events. For example, in 1966 Bob Kennedy went to Alabama and Mississippi—to the universities, but he went elsewhere. And he got a friendly reception. In a way, the stereotypes about the South helped a Kennedy, since many people thought of everything Southern as medieval and racist and reactionary. Hell, *somebody* was sending Kefauver and Gore and Yarborough to the Senate all these years, even though Gore and Yarborough lost in 1970. But because everyone thought Bob Kennedy was poison in the South, his reception there made news.

Lindsay could do the same thing. In Atlanta, which not long ago elected a liberal Jew and a liberal black man to its two top offices, he could well speak to a group about foreign policy and what it was doing to us domestically. He could go to a university, a law school, and a labor union meeting and talk to them, mostly answer questions. The national impact is clear: Lindsay's not afraid to leave his natural base; he'll talk to people, answer their questions. And if he has a rough time—if he gets yelled at or heckled—that's almost always a plus for a candidate because of that sense of fair play people still have about politics. It isn't right to shout somebody down when he's trying to speak. So if somebody calls Lindsay a son of a bitch, O.K., that's fine. He was there and he took it. He had the guts to go and talk issues, and that's the important thing in the beginning.

In all of these settings, Lindsay has to talk about key national issues—and it's far better for a man to say what he really thinks than to fudge it up. If a question is asked and Lindsay disagrees with the premise, he should say so and say why. It's the kind of thing Bob Kennedy did on college campuses when the problem of student draft deferments was raised. He'd say, "You're getting the unfair advantage while poor people are being drafted." It was blunt enough, straight enough so he could turn people around; and Lindsay did some of that in his mayor's race in 1969.

But the other part of this pre-campaign time is much deeper than any issues. To be brutally honest about it, whatever his program, people are more fascinated with a candidate as an individual than they are with his speech. Sure, the *New Republic* will have a forty-five-part story on whether guaranteed incomes are better than a negative income tax, but for the audience, the perceptions are smart, but very vague. Half the time a person couldn't tell you what a man said two minutes after he said it. Instead, they sit in some kind of awe of a charismatic figure. They think: "Gee, look at Bob Kennedy with ten kids. What a stud." Or: "He's young, but he sounds like he knows what he's talking about." Or: "How can they call him ruthless when he has such a kind smile?"

The fact is that a John Lindsay has that charisma. There was a reception for teachers at Gracie Mansion, where the mayor lives in New York, in the '69 campaign. Those teachers, less than a year before, were in a bitter strike and were ready to kill Lindsay. But they came and got their coffee, and were for the most part so flattered to be there at Gracie Mansion that they were beaming. No matter how cynical it may sound, you just can't discount good looks and charm and sex appeal. I'll stop being cynical about it when people stop voting because of it. Until then, it's a fact—and it's a fact that Lindsay's got it.

Sometime in 1971 Lindsay has to move explicitly toward the Democratic party. Lindsay endorsed Arthur Goldberg, the Democratic candidate, for governor of New York in 1970, against Rockefeller, whom Lindsay supported three times for President. By the 1970 campaign, Lindsay had already endorsed numerous Democrats in New York City for state, local, and Congressional offices. But as far as the Republicans go, Lindsay has to leave his Republicanism behind him. There is simply no future for him in that party. When you find yourself sandwiched in between Barry Goldwater, Strom Thurmond, John Wayne, Roman Hruska, and Spiro Agnew, it's time to leave.

But the worst thing Lindsay could do would be to court the "leaders" of the Democratic party. In the first place, they are simply not his constituency. Big labor, the senior Congressional leaders, the South— none of these elements of the party can be expected to be sympathetic to a Lindsay bid.

More important, the sources of Lindsay's strength are anathema to the leadership of the Democratic party—indeed, to either party. It's almost a feeling that if a man has independent political strength, he won't respond to party calls. Whatever the reason, the party "leadership" hasn't gone for the charismatic candidate since Eisenhower. Had it been left to them, John Kennedy wouldn't have won in 1960; they wouldn't have helped Robert Kennedy one bit in 1968 if he had gone to Chicago, and they turned their backs both on Rockefeller and Reagan in 1968 for the dependable, safe Richard Nixon.

The last thing in the world John Lindsay should or could do would be to run around the country quietly arranging deals with political leaders. It wouldn't work—and it would also work against the strength that Lindsay would bring to a Presidential race: the sense that he can pull the crowds, that he can win the affection of the people, that he can lead the ticket to victory.

So Lindsay has to show just enough concern with the Democrats, combined with a *real* showing of his strong pull in different kinds of constituencies. Let him "become" a Democrat (whatever that may mean) some time in 1971, let him endorse candidates from the progressive wing of the party—and while he's doing it, let him show the party leaders that he has the charisma, the impact, to turn out votes.

For party people in general—like the county chairmen in upstate New York, or most other places, for that matter—what really counts is: "who's gonna buy me the best dinner today? What have you done for me today?" There's a constant battle in trying to win over party leaders, and they tend to go to the highest bidder and the safest face. Even when a politician thinks he has them, he may find out differently tomorrow. So Lindsay has to do what John Kennedy did in 1960 and what Bob Kennedy was going to do in 1968. For JFK, the argument was: "The polls show I can win with the people. I'm taking the primary route, I'm going to prove I can win until you can't stop me."

After winning in California, RFK was going to blitz towns where the delegates or the leaders weren't going to go for him. He was planning to go into the shopping centers, into neighborhoods with motorcades, and he was going to show the delegates there that if they went to the convention without supporting Robert Kennedy, the people were really going to protest. In a sense, he was going to try to run primaries in the big non-primary states, by arguing that the people were responding to Kennedy. Why? Because he knew it was a waste of time to give a dinner to a delegate who could get a dinner from everybody else. He couldn't outpromise Hubert, so he would show these politicians that their future depended on support for Robert Kennedy. Polls alone can't do it. They have to *see* those crowds, which nobody else could get, that real enthusiasm which can't be staged or faked. And John Lindsay has the glamour in the pre-campaign stage to make people prick up their ears and pay attention.

One of the most important questions is. Would the Democrats turn to John Lindsay if there was anybody else? That isn't clear—but it's apparent that it's a dangerous game to go against the man who won most or all of the Presidential primaries. And the question is, how does Lindsay stack up against the other Democrats. Take a look at each of them.

Hubert Humphrey in 1972 will be the Democrats' Richard Nixon. He has no other way to go. He has to prove he's a winner and that he can win in the primaries. Humphrey can't prove anything by getting the leaders, because he had them in 1968 and he lost it. And, in an odd way, that need of Humphrey's is exactly what Lindsay needs. In 1968 Nixon beat nothing in New Hampshire—Romney had withdrawn before the primary—but the win was a plus factor. Since I think Lindsay could take Humphrey four ways from Sunday in a primary, Humphrey may find himself playing the role of sacrificial lamb to Lindsay.

Ironically, just as Lindsay has to be the John Kennedy of 1972, Ted Kennedy has to be the Lyndon Johnson of 1972, depending on the leadership for any Presidential ambitions he may have.

Teddy, much more than his brothers, is comfortable in the Senate—although probably a little less comfortable since losing the job of Senate Whip in January of 1971. So if—if—Ted Kennedy wanted to be President, I think he'd try to count on the senators and party leaders to control their delegations and create a draft movement. But I think that day is gone—you don't draft a person for President anymore. And since I don't think Ted Kennedy will want to go that primary route, will want to spend the twenty-four days on the trail, I think there will be no opposition from Ted Kennedy.

Senator Edmund Muskie, now the front-runner, was the luckiest guy in 1968. He was a good, bright, low-keyed guy running against five of the biggest stiffs ever to enter national races. Hell, Tom Dewey looks lovable next to Richard Nixon, and Martha Mitchell's demure if you put her next to Hubert. Add Wallace, LeMay, and Spiro and what have you got, beside a lot of doubts? You've got Ed Muskie. But there's nothing there that can draw people to him. I mean, you can try to push him as the thoughtful, quiet man; but Lindsay doesn't come across as hysterical, and neither does McGovern. Also, as long as we're getting into all these analogies, I think Muskie would become the Symington of 1972, looking for the party leadership to swing it for him on the notion that "he's everybody's second choice." (Just to round it out, I suppose Eugene McCarthy takes on the Stevenson role—rejected prophet.)

Senator George McGovern's problem is that he has not found the words to unite people behind him. He has a lot of things going for him—bluntness, honesty, and a lot more perception about Vietnam than almost anyone else on the national scene—and a lot earlier. But somehow I can't see McGovern taking the primaries, and the old-guard leadership isn't very hot on him. He, like Harold Hughes, would make a good second man on a Lindsay ticket, not just for geographic balance, but because he offsets the glamour image of Lindsay. But I don't see McGovern making it to the top.

The key to winning is a mix—it's part audacity and part very careful planning. I think Americans like a man who wants the job. All that talk from Stevenson in 1952 about the cup passing to worthier lips—that's hogwash. Everyone knows that you don't get trapped into running for President—either you want it and you go hard for it, or you don't want it and you back out. No politician who says he's not interested is telling the truth unless he takes a Sherman: "If nominated I will not run, if elected I will not serve." How many guys have you heard say that instead of: "Well, no, I am not a candidate, but I would say to those thousands of ordinary people urging me to run . . . "

So look at New Hampshire. I would say that before 1972—before any formal declaration of candidacy—Lindsay should go up to New Hampshire for a speech or two, maybe just a vacation, and a talk with a businessmen's or civic group. They will be receptive to listening to a man who's talked about for President—but the key is, *don't* try to build a crowd. First (some of that Nixon cynicism is useful), it may not be possible to do, and, if not, then the stories will come out about the failure of Lindsay to create any interest. Go up to New Hampshire for small, quiet discussions, and no one will need to make excuses for not supplying a crowd.

Second, there's a natural resentment against storming into a state like New Hampshire with thirty-five cameras and an enormous crowd of people. New Hampshire is New England—they can spot the hoopla very quickly. They want to hear a man talking for himself, with the ability to stand up by himself. So appearance on radio and TV, speeches, discussions—it should all be done very low-key. I would meet with some of those who count in New Hampshire commun- ities—business people, civic leaders—because if they get interested, they have a commitment to get others interested.

And I would hit the colleges. I said earlier that it would be important for Lindsay not to become the kids' candidate. But even with the resentment, I think adults like a Presidential candidate who can do what they can't: talk to their kids, argue with them, and retain some of their respect. In addition, especially with the high-school students, a politician gets a good picture of what their parents are thinking. Kids in high school, despite all the changes, still get their politics from home—and it's a good way to listen in secondhand to what's being talked about in the homes of New Hampshire people.

The rallies have to build slowly, toward momentum in the last week. This is the kind of state that can fool the experts—they said a month before the election in 1968 that McCarthy would be lucky to get 20 percent of the vote. And in fact he lost the bigger population centers, but he beat Johnson in the small towns, with his soft-spoken kids and low-key campaign. That's what Lindsay has to do—a long, long, low-keyed cam- paign: at the plant gate at 6 A.M., at the shopping centers at noon, into the main streets of villages at 5 P.M., talking, spending time with a few people with real problems. Because that's how you learn to listen to people—and listening is what makes for a better candidate and a better man.

In addition, Lindsay should meet—again, in small, private discussions—with the local press. You don't have to be Spiro Agnew to realize that a lot of people just don't trust the big press-TV sources for news. Their weekly papers are far more trustworthy, and they're important parts of the flow of information. In all these meetings, by the way, there is the added ad- vantage that the national press will stay out of New

Hampshire until the climax starts. They can't find anything visual in small meetings, and, more important, *Lindsay doesn't want them*. He has to learn about the state on his own first—that's the important step.

Now, with a week or two to go in New Hampshire, the excitement should be building, volunteers should be out ringing doorbells and talking about Lindsay. You can see here again that the worth of a man and his campaign success have a lot in common—if he can't generate this sense of excitement, if he can't reach the people, then why should *he be* President? But if he has—and I think Lindsay can—the last two weeks build to a sense of drama and importance about John Lindsay and the kind of leadership he represents.

Assume that Lindsay does well in New Hampshire —I'm not even sure what "do well" means, because if Muskie enters New Hampshire, Lindsay ought to be able to have himself labeled the underdog, what with Maine being right next to New Hampshire. But assume he wins. Wisconsin is obviously the next stop.

Wisconsin is the state where I grew up and where I started in political work; I think I know it, and it's a natural for Lindsay. There is a natural constituency for him in Madison, where the University of Wisconsin is (assuming it's still standing by 1972). Not just kids, but the faculty and graduate-student community should be a good base for Lindsay to start with. There are two papers—the *Capital Times* in Madison and the *Milwaukee Journal*—that have been against the war for quite a while and would be receptive to Lindsay. (When Lindsay went to Wisconsin in 1968 for Rockefeller, the *Capital Times* editorially suggested that Lindsay run himself. And when he spoke at the university, the kids cheered his attack on the war and booed his plug for Rocky—which shows that they still learn something in between the riots.) There's a large black population in Milwaukee which he should do well with, and there are union groups in factories all

over the state who should be feeling the real impact
of Nixon's economics by 1972.

Hell, I can outline for you right now a stop which
would show Lindsay's appeal *outside* his base, say, in
rural, northern Wisconsin. I'd pick Wausau. They've
got an airport, a TV station, and enough people to be
visible. I'd go fishing for a speaking invitation—probably before the New Hampshire primary, maybe even
before his announcement—and then I'd pull out the
stops for a real turnout, a crowd; and believe me,
liberal or conservative, they'd turn out for John Lindsay because he does have the glamour and the class,
and that's enough for Wausau to want to look at.
Curiosity, if nothing else, will turn them out. Who is
Lindsay? What is he? How does he talk? Is he as handsome as he looks on TV? I know that's not what they
teach in political science, but at the bottom line, that's
what people will come out to see.

Now with apologies to Women's Liberation, I would
organize an overall committee composed mostly of
women; they'd bring out the men. I'd probably have
two appearances in Wausau, and I'd have lots of publicity, lots of telephones ringing to invite people to
hear John Lindsay. I'd have an airport press conference, and I'd work for an airport crowd, so the cameras would catch people cheering for Lindsay and
reaching out to shake his hand. That initial TV impact
is *not* what he says; it's a single piece of information:
that John Lindsay is far away from his home base and
one of the biggest crowds in history has turned out to
see him and cheer him.

I'd try a number of angles. If it's in the middle of a
campaign, the mayor might let school out. How often
will Wausau see a man who may be President? People
know the stakes in a Presidency. Invite them to meet
Lindsay. Invite them to join up: We'd like you with
us now—before the bandwagon starts. That figured
critically in JFK's campaign—people thought he might
do it, they jumped aboard, and that movement *became*

the bandwagon. You can see how that kind of spirit could catch on at Wausau: this is our chance to make a difference, to get new leadership, and to be with a President on the ground floor.

And, in contrast to New Hampshire, I would emphasize excitement. Bands help that spirit, and there are dozens of high-school and CYO and Junior Legion Post bands that never get to play except for parades. I think they'd like the chance to play for a man who could be President of the United States. To be blunt, there are kids all over America whose mothers have hoped they will be models or dancers or on TV—they wouldn't pass this chance by.

And then the day—the Lindsay visit—becomes an event. People think nothing of traveling fifty miles to see a celebrity at an airport. Crowds could be pulled from four or five counties—I know, because we did it in 1959, with John Kennedy's Wisconsin stop in Marshfield. It becomes a day, an event, and then the momentum builds. I think I'd include a plant-gate appearance —and here, too, advance work is critical. It has to be a friendly union—like the UAW for Bob Kennedy when the national AFL-CIO was hostile. I'd find a plant with one entrance, not thirty, so you don't have Lindsay standing there with nobody filing by him to shake his hand. And I'd find a plant with a gate by the parking lot and bus stop, so Lindsay will see the day shift when they go in. It isn't that hard—but it's the kind of detail that political footwork is really all about.

After the plant-gate visit, I'd have a breakfast reception. Coffee, cake, handshaking in a high-school gym or a hotel room. The women would turn out, and so might the white-collar men. Lindsay is very good at the small, quiet talk, and it would make that personal contact work, that feeling that Lindsay isn't some New York pretty boy. Then I'd have a business luncheon—say, the Kiwanis. It's possible to have one group host a meeting and invite all the other social civic groups—or else a jointly hosted meeting where Lindsay gives a short speech and answers questions. You would also make it pointedly known—through the MC—that John Lindsay has addressed the largest such meeting in the history of the community.

In the afternoon I would have Lindsay at a senior citizens' home. Something that's visual, and also something that reminds a candidate of the people out there depending on him. Again, I keep reminding you of how politics and the right thing are often the same thing. It's good politics to have a man shown talking to the elderly, because there's a lot of guilt about the way we treat old people in America now, shunting them out of homes and into hospitals and holding-pens we call rest homes. It's also good to let a man know there are people counting on him, who need his help.

In the evening—beginning, say, around 7 P.M.—I'd have a reception. It's an ideal forum for a man like Lindsay, who's got glamour and whom people want the chance to meet and talk to. Fifty or so women should be designated as hostesses, with no hierarchy, otherwise all those at the bottom want to know why the others are at the top. Each of them invites twenty or thirty of her friends, and then you get a hall that holds about two thousand people. Make phone calls and, if there's time, send out invitations, because an invitation means something—it's a mark of significance, and it means the person who gets one is really likely to come.

Then that hall is jammed. People are waiting outside to meet Lindsay. There won't be any major foreign-policy statement. But the idea of a face-to-face meeting is really important. In a sense, the very idea of waiting an hour to shake John Lindsay's hand *means* the guy must have something. If he shows up late, and they wait an hour, that means something too. Bob Kennedy used to be furious when he ran late—hell, I did that to him on purpose. But you know what? People never got mad at Kennedy. And the rest of the country read that thousands of people waited in line. Wow, he's gotta have something.

That's the kind of day I'd run with Lindsay. The press sees crowds—the crowds sense that they're part of something exciting and important. And that's what goes on the TV and in the press while the intellectuals debate the last sentence on the first page of the speech. But the average voter, he sees excitement and enthusiasm, and *that's* what he wants to be a part of.

Wisconsin is relatively easy. Indiana is sheer murder for any liberal who is anti-war and cares about minorities. Bob Kennedy went into Indiana because he had to, to show he could win in hostile territory, where the Establishment was fighting him, and where the politics were considered Right. For Lindsay, it would be tougher. He's not Catholic. He's not the brother of a martyred President. He's anti-war and pro-black. The Indianapolis papers will be lying in wait for him, and the mayor of Indianapolis is Nixon's closest big-city friend.

Now the facts are that Lindsay doesn't have to go to Indiana. It wasn't a battleground until 1968, and there are enough primaries to choose from so he could stay out. But if Lindsay went for all the marbles, I would have him argue for fair play; in a way, you can get a long way by simply disarming people, in a personal, friendly campaign. I'm here because Indiana is important—they can make a judgment. Do I really look like some ogre from New York? Will you let me present my case to you? I'd go into the smallest towns possible, mixing with people, with a lot less hoopla than in Wisconsin, but, in a way, with a lot more reliance on his personality. Remember, you're going to have those papers in Indianapolis that will call Lindsay everything from a traitor to a child molester, and it's up to Lindsay to overcome that. And the way a guy like Lindsay does it is to disarm the myths. When Bob Kennedy stood on that train platform in 1968, kidding with the people, they may not have agreed with everything he said, but they knew he wasn't a monster from New York. Lindsay has that same thing.

I'll tell you something else. When it comes to winning a state like Indiana, you're dead if you turn Lindsay into a Stevensonian candidate, who's way above the people. He's got that tendency to preach just a little, and it could be deadly. If you get the intellectual crowd around him, if you think you can pull four thousand people from Indianapolis out of their homes to the War Memorial to hear John Lindsay pontificate, you're nuts. If a candidate can't show some empathy on issues, the audience will turn off. But for openers, that simple sex instinct is very powerful political stuff. If the candidate is a goddamn good-looking guy, the women will come out and drag the men out with them. There's a feeling around any glamour-candidate that maybe he could share a little of what he has. And what he says isn't all that important.

Hell, I would have been dead long ago if I could have screwed one-tenth of the women along the route of his motorcades who wanted to sleep with John Kennedy. Do you think they were jumping up and down because of his position on farm supports? No, there was a beautiful man. They'd say, "Gee, look at that guy. God, would I love to sleep with him."

That sense of personality will work on a man who's a good candidate—it will teach him how to relate to people. In 1959 John Kennedy wasn't all that good a speaker. Robert Kennedy in 1964, when he ran for the Senate, was simply terrible. But when a candidate begins to feel that affection from a crowd, when they show him they want to hear what he has to say, and why he wants to be President, the candidate begins to work out a five- or a ten- or a fifteen-minute talk. He opens up and answers questions. And so, again in a funny way, the stuff of sex appeal and crowd appeal can actually help a man to be a better candidate and a more candid one. It's all very strange.

In all this primary strategy, by the way, I don't discount TV. It's clearly the way people now learn about politics in America. But TV—commercials or news—still depends on what kind of guy a candidate is. I think most people still don't trust Nixon. They can light him properly for TV, put the right kind of make-up on him, but somehow it doesn't come across as honest. With a Lindsay, the TV would pick up the personal qualities *and* the crowd response, and then the momentum would carry things along. The crowds draw the TV coverage, the TV shows the enthusiasm, then the TV turns out more crowds, and the cycle goes on. The commercials are—even with the time limits—good places to move away from the hoopla and show the candidate talking to people, about issues. Even if a candidate can't explain everything, you can convey a tone, a sense of what you regard as important. Both Kennedy and McCarthy did that with their commercials in 1968, and it would be right for Lindsay too.

Of course, it's impossible to predict winners in primaries now. I'll leave that to the columnists who are always so sure of themselves, even when they're busy explaining why they were wrong about last week's elections. But it's pretty clear to me that an audacious, all-out campaign for John Lindsay has a good chance of winning a solid majority of the primaries. However, that isn't enough. Lindsay would have to win almost all of them. Looking at it with a lot of ifs and buts, I'd say Lindsay would run very strong in Wisconsin, Oregon, and California, have a shot at it in New Hampshire and Nebraska, and that Indiana would be his version of West Virginia—a state that would prove his strength if he could win that primary.

If Lindsay came out of the primaries with big wins, he'd then be in a position to try what Bob Kennedy was going to do in 1968: to storm the big non-primary states, to prove his pull, to say, "You may not like me, but the people do, and if you want to win this thing, you'd better come with me." By 1972, the traditions of politics may have fallen so far that even Lindsay's new-found Democratic bias may not hurt him too much. Also, the notion of an independent run for the Presidency just may get Lindsay a hearing from Democrats. And if the McGovern Commission reforms are in effect—if there is no unit rule at any level, and real participation by all the elements—I think Lindsay could come out of 1972 as the nominee of the Democratic party.

Presidents are human beings. Does that sound like a fairly obvious statement? Well, it isn't. Somehow we've gotten it into our heads that Presidents rule by divine right—that once they get elected everybody's supposed to shut up and bow. Well, in early 1960 I saw John Kennedy walk through the streets of Wisconsin towns at 6:30 A.M., looking for someone to shake hands with; and he sure was a human being then. And I saw him when he was President and hadn't slept right, or was going through rough times, and he was a human being then.

But the trappings we throw around a President—ruffles and flourishes, "Hail to the Chief," national TV when and where he wants it, and the sheer frightening power he has—can hypnotize people. On top of that, Richard Nixon is a man who really is nobody in particular; so when he runs in 1972, it's going to be one of the most sickening spectacles any President has ever pulled. You can see right now what it's going to be: wrapped in the American flag, surrounded by Bob Hope and Billy Graham and wounded war veterans, sending Spiro off to stir up the Yahoos, and trying to turn the election into a referendum on America vs. Communism, traitors, and sex perverts.

So one of the first things Lindsay would have to do would be to remind people that it's part of the American tradition to vote against incumbents who haven't done a good job. That can't be a part of a campaign, but when you think back, for example, to the 1930's, to movies like *Mr. Smith Goes to Washington,* you had the feeling then that politicians—even Presidents—deserved some close watching. You have to remind people that the President is chosen by them and could be retired by them.

Here again, a media campaign isn't enough. Nixon has very strong emotional support to rely on: fly the flag and "Support our boys in Vietnam." Lindsay has to keep that primary momentum and extend it—I mean go everywhere.

That's one of the keys to Lindsay beating Nixon— maybe *the* most important thing. He has to go to the people. He has to do it all: the crowds and the bands and the motorcades, the rallies, and the long question-and-answer sessions, the willingness to let everyone speak to him and to learn from the country.

Now there are two things Nixon could do. The first is what Johnson started doing late in 1967 and early in 1968, before he pulled out of the race. He could retreat into the White House, speaking at military bases, Medal of Honor ceremonies, prayer rallies and Jaycee conventions. Fine. In that case, Lindsay has a built-in argument: the President is afraid to face the people of the United States. He won't take his case to them. If Lindsay is in hostile territory, that's the pitch. "Look, I'm here, I'm listening to you, talking with you, because a President can't lead if he doesn't understand America. Where's Richard Nixon? Has he been here? Does he know the unemployment rate in this country is nine percent? Has he *done* anything except make speeches?" And gradually Lindsay could drive home the point that the President has lost touch. Of course it can be done, because it happened in 1968. Even before he announced that he was running for President, Kennedy would remind his audiences over and over that the President was unable to travel in his own country.

Oddly, you can turn the Agnew-TV argument against the President. "Why does Nixon hide behind television?

Why won't he come out and meet the people?" If the TV is showing an essentially passive Nixon and an active, driving Lindsay, that's the kind of contrast that Lindsay can play on. Likewise the debate thing. In 1968 Nixon was hurt by his refusal to debate. What he's likely to claim as President is that he would give away secrets. Hell, John Kennedy had already committed himself to debate his 1964 opponent. Let Lindsay go on that issue: "If Nixon is so unsure of himself that he'll spill out state secrets on TV, what kind of President is he?" People do not like hidden candidates —even when it's the President.

Nixon's advisers, as I've mentioned, know how to stage a personal campaign. They know how to create the image of excitement for TV. What does Lindsay do in that kind of situation?

Again, let me reach back to Robert Kennedy. When Johnson was President, during the 1966 Congressional campaigns, it wasn't LBJ who was the big draw—it was Kennedy. He could draw bigger crowds, more enthusiastic crowds. Johnson knew it—which is one reason, I think, why he ducked out of going to California. He had advance men all over the state reporting back to the White House that Kennedy's crowds could not be matched. And Johnson wasn't interested in news reports of Kennedy outdrawing the President in the nation's biggest state.

Say that Nixon pulls his 1968 stunts. Say they put up the sawhorses for three blocks and create the bussed-in, manufactured crowds. Lindsay can *go right back into that same city* and outpull Nixon. Don't put the barricades up for three blocks; build a three-mile motorcade—it can be done. Unless the press is totally asleep at the switch, they'll begin to spot the difference. Remember that in 1968 most of the press liked Humphrey. It's just that he gave them nothing to compare with Nixon's phoniness. It was a phony Nixon crowd vs. a nonexistent Humphrey crowd, and Nixon came out on top.

But if you have Lindsay drawing five to ten thousand people in a long motorcade, and Nixon's doing it in a five-block area, you've got your story. Hell, in '68 even the press guys who wanted to do a hatchet job on Nixon had no angle. They were dying to show up Nixon's phony campaign, but there was no contrast. Lindsay, if he ran it right, could build that contrast. In 1960, when Nixon found the crowds going to Kennedy, he tried to duplicate those motorcades, and it was a bust. The morale went, and the pendulum, that sense of which way a campaign's going, began shifting to John Kennedy. Think of that in '72. The President is losing support. They're coming to hear Lindsay. There's a thirst for new leadership. Boy, if that kind of momentum starts building, Lindsay can take it all.

Now let's look briefly at two other basic problems for Lindsay: one, the blue-collar worker, and two, the whole patriotism bit.

In New York City, Lindsay is poison in blue-collar areas; and the anti-Lindsay quality of many of the hardhat demonstrations have probably communicated themselves out to other parts of the country. What can Lindsay do? The same thing John Kennedy did with the Protestant ministers. He has to go right into those factories, and to those construction sites, and talk it out. It's entirely possible that by '72 the economy will have wiped out the resentment about Lindsay being too kind to blacks and kids. I watch these hardhats bragging about their patriotism, but when was the last time they didn't strike a missile plant or defense site when the issue was money? No, I think money is the key issue, and if we still have a recession-inflation, or if we have a depression by '72, they'll turn off a lot of that anti-Lindsay stuff.

And Lindsay simply has to be there more than Nixon. That's the point. He has to get yelled at, get a feeling for that blue-collar worker, so that when he talks about their problems, it's not book-learned, it's for real. He showed something of that in '69, when he kept going into Brooklyn and Queens, into civic centers and synagogues. I think the blue-collar vote for Nixon is soft—and with the economy in trouble, I think it's totally up for grabs.

As it happens, that patriotism argument can be turned around by Lindsay. First, with those who support the war, there's a strong feeling that it was a mistake and that all that money could have been better spent at home. That was Lindsay's pitch as mayor in the '69 campaign: that all our city's tax money was going for nothing. That argument on a national scale makes sense—and it has surprising strength even among the patriotic groups. It's my country and my tax money, damnit, and why is it going to all those crooks in Saigon?

Second, there's Lindsay's war record. There's a conviction among heartland Americans that the anti-war argument is really a disguise for cowardice—that people like Humphrey who were never in the military are weak, that the kids who protest are just trying to get out of doing their duty. As it happens, Lindsay saw combat in World War II—he has a few battle stars to his credit. And I tell you, nothing shuts up hecklers faster than that: "No one questioned my loyalty when I was on that beach in World War II. These battle stars didn't come because of any fear or disloyalty. I say this war has to end for the sake of our country and our sons and our treasure." There is resentment when a man toots his own horn. But when he uses his war record to counterpunch, it's a strong argument.

We come, I suppose, to the key question: Can Lindsay beat Nixon? My answer, looking a good way ahead, is yes.

Remember, Nixon's Southern strategy depends on his winning the Midwest and California to win. Nixon barely beat Humphrey in Ohio, Illinois, and California. In '72 the economy could sweep all three of those "battleground" states into the Democratic column, especially with the idea of a new, exciting candidate like Lindsay.

Furthermore, the very glamour of a Lindsay has an attraction in the heartland states. Take Iowa. For some reason, both Kennedys did very well in Iowa. Maybe it's glamour, or the sense of strength in leadership. But I think Lindsay would have that kind of appeal there too. If you remember that in most Midwest states there's a good deal of industry, if you put that together with the unhappiness about the war and the hope of something better, I think the Nixon policy of offering up symbols will not take the place of a bread-and-butter campaign that brings to it the voice of a man who was against the war even five years ago.

If you put Lindsay in that arena—drive him from January to November with his strength and looks and impact—I think Lindsay would win. I give him most of the Northeast—New York, Pennsylvania, Connecticut, Massachusetts, Rhode Island, maybe New Jersey. I give him California in a tough race. I give him Minnesota and Michigan, with a shot at Ohio and Illinois. And that's most of what he needs. If the breaks come his way, Lindsay can do it. It's a long shot now, but I've seen fights a lot tougher. So if I had to put money on it, I'd say that on January 20, 1973, the guy with his hand on the Bible will be John V. Lindsay.

Index